Contents

streets
ahead

Design Council
in association with the
Royal Town Planning Institute

28 Haymarket London SW1Y 4SU

Streets Ahead

First edition
published in the United Kingdom 1979 by
Design Council, 28 Haymarket, London SW1Y 4SU

Printed in England by
Jolly & Barber Limited, Rugby

Designed by Betty Dougherty

ISBN 0 85072 081 8

Introduction

The quality of the street environment can have almost as much effect on people's lives as the quality of their own homes. A residential road with little traffic and lots of trees obviously creates the kind of peaceful atmosphere in which most people would prefer to live. Shopping can be agreeable in a well planned precinct which is well served by transport and has thoughtfully placed seats and other amenities; or it can be a nightmare of dragging children through overcrowded pavements or dodging cars and lorries. Public gardens and parks can be properly maintained and attractive, or near-derelict targets for vandals. Playgrounds can provide safe entertainment for children, or they can be so badly designed and maintained as to be positively dangerous. Signposting can be well designed, well sited and therefore helpful, or it can be battered, ugly and confusing. Poster hoardings can mask unsightly buildings or mar a pleasant view.

This book aims to help everyone involved in creating the street scene, from the planners, engineers, architects and designers who work for the local authorities and public utilities to the shopkeepers and businessmen who are responsible for the facades of their own buildings, and the individuals, amenity societies and pressure groups who are simply interested in improving and protecting the environment of their own neighbourhood.

The book has two major themes. First, it examines some of the fundamental developments that are changing the street scene quite dramatically in many parts of the world – changes that range from the reversal of traditional vehicle/pedestrian priorities, which has given a totally new look to certain residential areas, to the belief in some declining industrial areas that the task of tackling the visual and environmental harm caused by industry is at least as important as dealing with unemployment or other economic ills.

Second, the book looks at the individual components that go to make up the street scene. For it realises that the quality of the street environment relies as much on the design, selection and siting of such items as paving, lighting, litter bins, seats, planting and fencing as on overall town design policies and grand improvement schemes; that day-to-day cleaning and maintenance are as important as fine plans and quality materials; and that the workmen who actually put up signs and plant gardens have as much effect on the end result as the senior architect or town planner of the local authority.

Streets, parks and shopping precincts are essential parts of people's living space. As such they must function well and be pleasant, and this demands awareness, flexibility and care on the part of those responsible to ensure that the results of individual changes on the overall appearance and effectiveness of these public places are satisfactory.

Streets throughout the world

Interesting developments in the street scene are occurring in many parts of the world. This visual survey shows some of the more interesting schemes in Europe and North America.

Picture sequence
1 2
3 4
5 6

There are many ways of achieving a pleasant street, but one essential ingredient is that everything should be on a human scale and related in character.

Samarkand (1) uses well maintained gardens and attractive paving to soften some monolithic buildings. Both this street in Riga (2) and the square in Amsterdam (3) are pleasant and unspoiled by extraneous street furniture or other intrusions. Apart from the unfortunate road sign, this square in Gråbrødretory, Denmark (4) is unspoiled too, with the paving emphasising its informality. A mixture of old and new works well in the Järntorget Square in Göteborg, Sweden (5), while the new River Park in Chicago (6) demonstrates how appropriate scale between the various elements creates an attractive area.

6

BOB KINDRED

BOB KINDRED

Decorative features are important elements in the street scene. Water has always fascinated: this waterfall in Greenacre Park, New York (7 and 8), adds considerably to the relaxing atmosphere of a tiny city park. A series of small roof domes visually link the various items in the Kungsportsplatsen major bus/tram stop in Göteborg (9 and 10). Vandalism is a major problem in areas such as subways, stairwells, and car parks. Murals have been found to be an effective solution, both livening up a dull area and discouraging graffiti. This subway in the Greyfriars Centre at Ipswich (11) has been greatly improved by a mural (12) painted by students of the Suffolk School of Art.

GÖTEBORG CITY COUNCIL

GÖTEBORG CITY COUNCIL

BOB KINDRED

BOB KINDRED

The emphasis in urban planning in recent years has favoured the pedestrian, with schemes ranging from the complete pedestrianisation of shopping areas to the redesign of residential streets to benefit people on foot. Stuttgart has tackled both: in one of the old suburbs (13) a main street has been re-paved to be shared by pedestrians and vehicles, while in the main business area traffic has been completely replaced by shoppers and people strolling or listening to musicians. Pedestrians in New York now have their own walk-through waterfall (14).

Minneapolis is one of a number of American cities undergoing massive change, centred on Nicollet Mall (17). Here small buses provide transport while most vehicles are kept out. Nicollet Mall is bordered on both sides by outdoor plazas and courtyards, and features a multi-storeyed Crystal Court which, being covered, is a year-round town square alive with leisure and retail activities.

Great care has been taken to make the area as attractive by night as by day (18). In contrast is the Peavey Plaza (16, previous page), where fountains, stepped lawns, and trees provide a haven from the adjacent hustle.

MINNEAPOLIS CONVENTION AND TOURISM COMMISSION

MINNEAPOLIS CONVENTION AND TOURISM COMMISSION

GERALD SMART

JOHN FIELD

DESIGN COUNCIL

GERALD SMART

Pedestrianisation schemes have enhanced life in many towns and cities throughout the world. The choice of paving and street furniture can make or mar such schemes: in Essen (19) and Ottawa (20) the paving relates well to the colour and ambience of the surrounding buildings, while the decorative features such as the display cases and the fountain are appropriately subdued. Equally appropriate to the overall setting is the rather more colourful paving in the centre of Hereford (21). Limited access for public transport and some other vehicles is sometimes necessary in areas that are basically meant for pedestrians, and paving can perform a useful function in warning both drivers and pedestrians of possible conflict. Thus in Rotterdam (22) stripes mark a roadway between pedestrian areas, while in Exeter (23) a change in surface colour first indicates a prohibition to all but certain types of vehicle and then a second change combined with a width constriction warns of pedestrians crossing. The subtle two-colour grey paving in New London, Connecticut (24), sets off the white kerbing, shelters, lighting columns and the green of the grass and trees.

CHRIS SWANN/FRANCIS BRIDGEMAN

THE INSTITUTE FOR ENVIRONMENTAL ACTION INC. NEW YORK

10

Compared with many improvement schemes in the United States, most in Britain are simple and relatively inexpensive. The best are restrained, uncluttered and are in complete sympathy with their surroundings. Excellent examples are the little courtyard (25) off the recently pedestrianised square in the small Yorkshire town of Ossett and the High Street (26) in Corsham, Wiltshire. Equally attractive is the Black Lion scheme (27) at Honiton in Devon, where even the shop sign fits in with the overall cool elegance. Mildenhall in Suffolk is another small market town, and its new shopping precinct (28) well matches the older part of the town, with paving, lighting, planting and a small advertising drum providing additional visual interest. Pontefract (29) is another Yorkshire town that has pedestrianised its main street in a way that enhances its architecture (see also page 19), Hereford (30) is also basically attractive (see also page 10), but some details – such as the clutter of different styles of telephone kiosk and the unused cycle blocks – need attention.

DESIGN COUNCIL.

DESIGN COUNCIL.

A number of elegant footbridges have been designed in recent years, of which one is this suspension design in Warrington (31). But smaller-scale items are just as important: these seats under cover in the square at Pontefract have provided a meeting place for local people for generations.

The renovation of decaying buildings often offers opportunities for using modern materials and products to improve the surrounding area. At Washington New Town an old farm (33) has been converted into an attractive arts centre (34).

PHOTO-MAYO LTD

PHOTO-MAYO LTD

West Yorkshire is notable for some extensive pedestrianisation schemes, of which that in Ossett is outstanding (35). Previously (36), cars and pedestrians fought for space, with the inevitable railings, signs and strange mixture of lighting columns spoiling the attractive town hall vista. (See also the picture on page 11). Another old area that has been attractively renovated is this small courtyard in Marlborough, Wiltshire (38). Traditional paving and sympathetic shop signs add to the scene.

The design of street furniture in Britain tends to be utilitarian. Not so elsewhere, as is shown by the lighting, seats and traffic lights at Place Carnot, near Lyons in France (37).

BOB KINDRED

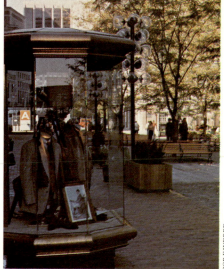

BOB KINDRED

DESIGN COUNCIL

BOB KINDRED

BOB KINDRED

THE INSTITUTE FOR ENVIRONMENTAL ACTION INC. NEW YORK

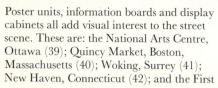

MICHAEL MIDDLETON

GLENROTHES DEVELOPMENT CORPORATION

DESIGN COUNCIL

Poster units, information boards and display cabinets all add visual interest to the street scene. These are: the National Arts Centre, Ottawa (39); Quincy Market, Boston, Massachusetts (40); Woking, Surrey (41); New Haven, Connecticut (42); and the First Chicago Centre, Illinois (43). Decorative paving can be important too: Fresno, California (44); Lisbon (45); and Glenrothes (46). Finally, coloured surfaces can be purely functional: in London's Kensington (47) they indicate a bus lane.

14

Improving the urban environment

by Gerald Smart, Professor of Urban Planning and Head of the Bartlett School of Architecture and Planning, University College London. Formerly County Planning Officer for Hampshire County Council.

'In the Strathclyde Region of Scotland, which includes Glasgow, 30 per cent of the housing has a poor environment, and most of this is extremely poor; 68 per cent of these areas are primarily in public ownership; only 55 per cent are known to have programmes for internal or external improvement.'

'In North West England the urban environmental problem, resulting from a combination of physical, social and financial factors, has one characteristic found wherever it occurs: there is a state of inertia which swamps those forces which normally ensure active maintenance and quick redevelopment. It can be seen throughout the region in the costs of pollution from industry, too often tolerated in the interest of survival of that industry; in areas of industrial obsolescence and no commercial pressure, where old buildings stand empty or partially used; and in areas which have been cleared of slums but which lack money for redevelopment.'

'In West Yorkshire, in the opinion of many residents, the quality of the environment is the most widespread and intractable problem facing the county. Poor environment is evident not only in the inner areas of the main cities and towns, but also in the smaller settlements. Often these same areas suffer from serious social and economic deprivation. Existing policies have helped to ameliorate the problems, but greater effort and more public and private resources are needed if any significant impact is to be made in the foreseeable future.'

'In inner London there needs to be a large continuing programme for the renewal of the urban fabric. This should take a different form from earlier programmes, but represents a challenge to the construction industry, architects and builders. Rebuilding and improvement to a more intimate scale; modernisation and remodelling of old estates inside and out; conservation and conversion to new uses of old buildings; development of a programme of small open spaces for multi-use; street improvement and tree planting. Owners and tenants will need to make a bigger contribution than before. All this will lead to a more varied and interesting street scene.'

So run some official statements about the conditions in which the population of our great urban areas live. These are just a selection. How do people themselves regard their environment? Surveys in the early 1970s in Liverpool and West Yorkshire suggest that it is the nuisances such as litter, rubble, smells, vandalism and noise which people in general are most concerned about. Very much part of the street scene, but an

Portsmouth's city centre (below) is only one focus of its environmental improvement effort, which strikes a balance between public preferences and the city's need to develop employment, tourist and recreational opportunities in what is a densely built up area. The new Civic Office site is seen here before and after redevelopment.

CITY OF PORTSMOUTH

CITY OF PORTSMOUTH

This diagram is based on one published by the Merseyside County Council showing the overall 'importance' of environmental problems as seen by respondents to their 1973 Household Interview Survey. The ranking takes account of the incidence and severity of problems; the importance of each problem is shown in terms of its distance from the average importance for all problems. The prominence of the three problems of vandalism, dirt or smells, and high bus or train fares is accounted for partly by the fact that they are experienced by widely differing groups of people every day.

Vandalism

Dirt or smells

Bus and train fares

Play areas
Small parks

Choice of homes

Employment
Building condition
Sports
Traffic

Home too small
Parking

Appearance

Household facilities
Evening entertainment
AVERAGE   Public transport

Noise

Medical services
Shops
Parks

Schools
Accessibility
Job security

Garage
Privacy
Roads
Rent, mortgage repayments

Dangerous buildings

A garden/people

Home too large
Area
Insecurity of tenure

Choice of tenure

Service for elderly handicapped
Further education
Sharing
Maternity services

RANK ORDER

aspect of it which tends to be concentrated in areas of generally poor environment, and thus needs to be tackled along with other improvements, aimed at solving the problems which the official statements so clearly express.

This article is about how some local authorities are approaching the job of improving their external physical environment; its appearance, safety, convenience, freedom from pollution and nuisance and so on. From varying standpoints, they see the task of civilising the environment as one of the greatest social responsibilities for the remainder of this century. They know that they are often fighting a losing battle against obsolescence, and many of them would like more money for the task (their bids to government for money, for housing especially, tend to work out at up to twice what their individual shares of the national cake might be). So they have some difficult decisions of priorities. Above all, they must have an eye to what can be done immediately, effectively, and at low cost. This calls for a high degree of determination and imagination.

For example, Rochdale, a Borough in Greater Manchester County with one of the worst legacies of obsolescence from the Industrial Revolution, has cut out much traditional red tape. In addition to its normal spending on housing rehabilitation and a pioneering effort in renewing a nineteenth-century industrial area beside a disused canal, it has set aside one per cent of the Borough rate – £375,000 per annum – for general environmental improvement. It also encourages each councillor to draw up to £1,000 from the rate fund for projects to be carried out in his or her ward by local community associations. An original and pragmatic approach to the setting of priorities, about which I shall be saying more later.

Wakefield, a city in West Yorkshire formed in 1974 by the amalgamation of 13 separate councils, and thus needing to create a new image, has given priority to schemes with a wide impact. These include the pedestrian precincts it and the West Yorkshire County Council have created in three of its main centres (costing £550,000 in all), in addition to its programmes of housing and improvement of the environment and degraded land, and to its spending on landscape and on conservation areas – a total (for environmental improvement) of £2 million out of a budget of £20 million. It regularly invites suggestions for projects throughout its district from councillors, amenity societies, and members of the public, and it runs an annual design award. No time-consuming, sophisticated analyses of need; but they get results.

And in South Yorkshire, the Metropolitan County Council has designated a series of 'environmental priority areas' in its structure plan, where problems of pollution, dereliction, open space shortage, poor housing, traffic disturbance, etc occur together – for example in the heavily industrialised and polluted Don and Dearne valleys at Sheffield, Rotherham and Barnsley. Gradually it intends to concentrate in these the large amounts which it is now spending on environmental improvement (£2 million per annum, which is about 18 per cent of its total capital budget). I shall return to this, too, later. Incidentally, the same highly selective approach is being followed in some other Metropolitan Counties, both in terms of expenditure and through the use of planning powers to steer new development towards the priority areas.

These examples are among the best, but they are not untypical. Before developing them further, however, let me first set out more of a context. Some problems of environmental improvement need solutions which, to be effective, have to be applied over a wide area. One might call them 'strategic'. These include those whose impact is relatively widespread, or

The Greater Manchester Borough of Rochdale has made strenuous efforts to improve obsolescent industrial buildings and, in particular, the nineteenth-century canal-side environment (above left and below). Small-scale residential housing rehabilitation schemes (above right) have also been encouraged, as have projects carried out by local community associations.

The City of Wakefield has put a premium on schemes with a wide impact in order to establish a new, favourable corporate image. This pedestrianisation scheme (above and right) is one of three such projects. Ten per cent of the annual budget is currently spent on environmental improvement.

whose solutions lie in the hands of several agencies (eg local authorities, government departments and nationalised industries); or they may require funds, staff and equipment beyond the local capacity. Here the choice of priorities should generally be made at the level of the region or conurbation. Such being the way of bureaucracy, as things stand at present, there may be no clearly made choice at this level between the different types of programme required – more money for pollution control, for example, as distinct from traffic management. Nevertheless, levels of expenditure can be and are gradually influenced by pressure from local authorities, although it is easier to find room to manoeuvre within the individual programmes (derelict land, for instance), giving priority to this area or to that.

Many environmental problems are nevertheless primarily 'local' in character, although the money available for them, like most other local expenditure, is not determined entirely by the local authorities themselves. These problems are ones which essentially concern local communities, with choices and solutions lying primarily within their own initiative, such as the improvement of housing and industrial areas, the conservation of historic buildings, pedestrianisation of shopping centres, tree planting and greenery, clutter and litter campaigns, etc. Here with an active and community-minded council, the amount of effort can be increased considerably when trade associations and voluntary groups are involved in the whole process, from choice to completion of the tasks themselves. But since the worst strategic and local environmental problems tend to coincide in areas of general deprivation, including unemployment, some kind of co-ordinating mechanism may well be necessary between county and district councils, or with government departments and other statutory agencies. Local authorities are best placed to take the initiative in this, and it is in their interest, as elected councils, representing the people of their area, to do so. Furthermore, a good scheme, properly co-ordinated, is likely to collect more for the local community by way of additional funds which are now available from many sources (including the EEC), and resources of manpower from the Job Creation Programme.

So in the areas of greatest need, environmental improvement will often have to be a combined operation; a challenge to local political leadership and organising ability. But it is a challenge that is increasingly being taken up in the big conurbations, where the need for environmental improvement comes a close second to, or even equal first with, the improvement of economic prospects.

Having set the scene, let me now describe the way in which some local authorities set about the job as a totality, so that we can see how the kind of improvements advocated in this book fit in.

Portsmouth is a city of 200,000 population in the prosperous urban area of South Hampshire; but it is a city with a difference. As an historic naval base it grew rapidly in the nineteenth century on its island site, and is now the most densely built-up urban area in southern England, and nationally second only to some of the Lancashire mill towns. Its legacy includes serious problems of obsolescence, a high level of unemployment, and some areas of multiple deprivation. Portsmouth has a strong political commitment to environmental improvement, both for the sake of its residents and to make it more attractive to employers.

The City Council's strategy is to concentrate effort and expenditure on General Improvement Areas (of which there are 10 to date, with a total of 6,000 dwellings); on its 19 Conservation Areas; on other deprived areas of pre-war housing, mostly in Council ownership; on the city centre; on major features in urban fabric (especially the environs of the M275 spur road, and other green areas which help to identify parts of the city); and on major environmental health measures (half the city is within smokeless zones, and increasing use is made of noise control areas).

Within this general strategy, priorities are determined mainly on an opportunity basis, without much recourse to techniques such as environmental evaluation or forecasting of obsolescence. Opportunities arise primarily through the capital works programme, and they are judged in the light of known public preferences (for better roads, pavements, street lighting, public cleansing) and choices expressed by councillors (eg a bold scheme for patterned paving on the promenade, in the economic interest of the City as a tourist and recreation area). The three-year 'environmental budget', largely focused on specific improvements to townscape and landscape in these areas, is £3.25 million over three years. In addition some £400,000 is spent each year on other improvements including

pedestrian precincts, rear service roads, £375,000 on grants for house improvement, and £6,000 on Historic Building Grants.

Portsmouth has a corporate framework for its management, but in addition to the usual committees, two special committees have 'roving commissions' in strategy for, and implementation of, environmental improvement. These set guidelines for other committees, pressurise other agencies (such as the County Council), and take their own initiatives from time to time. The public are involved through residential committees in each housing improvement area, on which ward councillors and leaders of community groups sit. And schools are brought in to assist with schemes like tree planting.

I now turn to a very different part of the country, Merseyside, whose metropolitan county council and five district councils serve a population of 1.5 million. Merseyside's strategy is to guide investment to the urban part of the county, enhancing the environment, encouraging housing and economic expansion on the county's 3,500 hectares of derelict and disused sites. There is a reciprocal policy of countryside

South Yorkshire County Council's capital environmental budget totals £2 million, and a further £1 million is spent annually on waste disposal. The demolition of the twin cooling towers overshadowing Rotherham town centre (above) cost £430,000 – a large proportion of this total, but a massive declaration of intent on the Council's part. Complete pedestrianisation of this area of Pontefract, in West Yorkshire (below) has resulted in a great improvement in amenity.

19

Nautical relics are featured in the remodelling of Queen Street in the Portsea area of Portsmouth to echo its long naval connections.

New planting and paving under construction in King Street, Portsmouth.

Merseyside has directed investment towards its urban areas, including inner Liverpool, but reclaiming despoiled land is a high priority throughout the county.

conservation. Although the County Council has a strongly corporate approach to its task, it is aware, first and foremost, of the inter-corporate dimension of Merseyside's problems. The District Councils take a pride in planning and in action for environmental improvement in their individual areas, but the County Council is very active in advocating the economic and environmental needs of the county as a whole (for example, additional resources towards housing rehabilitation and clearance, and general environmental improvement). It also provides a consultative forum for action on strategic problems, such as air and water pollution. The time may come when the environmental programme in its Structure Plan assumes equal importance to its programme for economic development.

At the present attention is focused on how to improve the prospects, in total, of the inner area of Liverpool, under the guidance of a 'partnership' committee set up between the Liverpool City Council and Central Government as a result of the Government's White Paper *Policy for the Inner Cities*. This is primarily an economic and social programme, but as might be expected, much of its expenditure will benefit the environment. The City Council has already reviewed unused land in the inner area. It believes that a major solution to the problem would require about £150 million to be spent, to which its current budgets contribute less than a quarter. It will be a long haul, but the partnership scheme has brought a more optimistic outlook.

In the wider county, first priority in the campaign for environmental improvement is to reclaim despoiled land and obsolete buildings, on which the county spends about £800,000 per annum. This includes litter abatement campaigns, because litter tends to concentrate in such situations. The second priority is to encourage more to be done to improve air quality, by means of smoke control, especially in areas of poor quality housing. Smoke control already operates in half the urban area of the county, but the earliest date by which other priority areas could be completed would be 1985. Third priority is to advocate further improvement on the condition of water-courses, especially the Mersey Estuary and its odour problems, which are the result of large quantities of untreated sewage. Although studies of the county's urban fabric are not yet complete, it is thought that with an increase in the already large expenditure on housing, and some further attention to the improvement of industrial areas, these priorities should go a long way towards meeting the strategic needs of the urban environment, and thus providing a framework for numerous programmes of local treatment. But the fact remains that the condition of the inner city environment is deteriorating faster than current rates of expenditure can improve it.

Over towards the Pennines one can learn much from the Greater Manchester area. Here, Bolton (with a population of 264,000) has its Borough Plan, which is a plan for the whole work of the Council rather than merely for its physical planning responsibilities. This is regularly revised and brought up to date as the basis for the various committee programmes. The plan says: '. . . obsolescence in the Borough is now approaching the level at which massive physical repair costs are outweighing the temporary advantages provided by obsolete accommodation, and this obsolescence produces highly damaging environmental effects'.

An 'attack on obsolescence' is therefore the Borough's main strategic aim. The plan boldly sets out environmental objectives (pollution control, derelict land recovery, leisure provision, conservation of landscape and historic buildings) and further social objectives (eg employment and housing) which relates to them. Within this, the Council's environmental priorities are: first, to start to tackle the largest area of industrial obsolescence in Greater Manchester, much of which is beyond their means; second, to maintain the momentum on housing clearance and building, but to encourage more take-up of housing improvement grants so that targets of 15,000 private houses improved by 1980 (16 per cent of whole borough housing stock) can still be met, in addition to the modernisation of 7,500 Council dwellings; third, to press on with smoke control, which is good value for money; and, fourth, to step up the derelict land programme, which has been running at about three quarters of the desired rate, although supported by 100 per cent government grants. Out of a total capital budget of £93m for the next three years, £86 million represents the projects which contribute to the 'attack on obsolescence'.

Bolton, a Council with strong political leadership and a corporate approach to their work, has achieved much despite frank misgivings about its ability to meet its targets. Its efforts have been recognised in Times Awards for housing improvement and for conservation; and by the completion in 1973 (including the construction of a new road) of a very successful pedestrianised town centre after four years of preparation.

In Rochdale, to which I referred earlier, the Borough Council's corporate strategy for the environment focuses on a vigorous programme of 'community based action areas', for housing and for general improvement of its nineteenth-century industrial legacy. These two programmes are interrelated, and of vital importance to the social, economic and physical wellbeing of the area. Its ideas on industry are home grown, so to speak, worked up from an experimental start in 1976. It aims at a gradual re-structuring of the environment rather than merely cosmetic treatment. The industrial improvement area consists of 110 acres of buildings such as old mills, accommodating 100 firms and 3,000 workers, surrounded by housing which is due to be cleared and from which more industrial land could be obtained. The fabric itself and the infrastructure both need rehabilitation, but industry must not be driven out in the course of this: a very single-minded priority scheme taking its

Bolton's achievements include a very successful town centre pedestrianisation scheme (top) and also housing improvement and renovation work (right) which has gained awards.

place within the integrated planning and implementation of all the Council's environmental improvements. Rochdale regards itself as 'a very poor borough, spending objectively, as much on industry as housing, and making good use of grants'. Indeed it has recently obtained a grant of £80,000 from the EEC for the provision of infrastructure.

The borough's organisation is interesting – almost unique in its streamlining. Seven members of its main committee meet weekly as a Control of Expenditure Board. For the Crawford Street industrial area itself there is a special Standing Committee of local authority members and industrialists, whose responsibility is to produce a plan, apportion costs, and oversee implementation. The Standing Committee is aided by two planners full time, and many other staff part time, including a psychologist; also by a Town Improvement team of 24 youngsters from the Job Creation Programme, supervised by an engineer, which is proving to be a good method of entry into permanent jobs.

Two years is a short time to show much in the way of results, but a plan has been agreed upon, a developer is building new factories on part of the area, and a start is being made on improving the remainder, for which industrialists are getting together, cleaning up, painting and rendering walls, supported by grants from the Council and from the Urban Aid programme. The Council is providing parking, cul-de-sac factory access (amidst much controversy), suggested colour schemes, graphics etc. A working party with the advertising industry is looking at the role of outdoor advertising. The disused canal is being reclaimed by one of the biggest Job Creation Programme projects in the UK (£0.5 million). The team have even set up their own anti-vandalism patrol.

I have one more example, this time on the other side of the Pennines, in South Yorkshire. When it was first established in 1974 the South Yorkshire County Council, to which I have already referred, decided to give very great priority to environmental improvement. The county is a highly industrialised one, with a well known legacy of pollution, dereliction and obsolete urban fabric, and with a strong political commitment to regeneration. To guarantee quick results it set up an Environment Committee, served by an Environment Department with 114 staff, responsible for waste disposal (one million tonnes of domestic and commercial waste per annum, and four million tonnes of industrial waste) and for formulation and implementation of the County's environment improvement programme. This committee is separate from the Planning Committee (and the Planning Department), but the two act closely together. Such is the enthusiasm that the Committee are planning their own weekend 'work-in' with pick-axes, shovels and young trees to plant.

The County Council prepares an annual corporate and financial plan, within which are co-ordinated its various programmes such as transportation, economic development, environmental improvement. It admits that its approach is somewhat opportunist at present, but it is gradually being recast in line with the priority areas, to which I have already referred, in other words towards a concentration of effort in areas defined as a result of problem analysis, and public and local authority opinion surveys. Within these areas, special priority is given to sites (including small ones) adjoining industry, communications and housing; also to collaborate efforts to reduce air and water pollution. As in the case of Merseyside, its work is complementary to that of District Councils such as Sheffield and Rotherham, which have much to show in experience and achievement.

Out of its 'environmental' budget of £2 million (not includ-

ing £1 million spent on waste disposal) the biggest single items are for derelict land reclamation for industry, open space or agriculture, on which it spends £500,000 or more on individual schemes. These qualify for 100 per cent government grant. Another large item has been the demolition of the twin cooling towers overshadowing Rotherham town centre, costing £430,000. Other items of importance include the giving of 50 per cent grants (up to £20,000) for small environmental improvement schemes by industrialists; other small grants (also underwritten to 50 per cent by the Countryside Commission) to farmers for landscaped upgrading; small grants-in-aid to voluntary groups (such as the Naturalists Trust, community action groups, etc); and for a programme of small nature reserves in school sites, costing £250 each. Grants for historic buildings amount to £7,000 per annum.

A particular feature of the organisation for 'getting things done' is the County Council's liaison with large organisations such as the NCB (who produce 12 million tonnes of colliery waste per annum) British Steel Corporation, British Rail, the Regional Water Authority and the Alkali Inspectorate. They support small voluntary groups who are active at weekends in conservation and environmental improvement. This voluntary work costs them £15,000 each year in materials, administrative support etc, and their contact with bodies like voluntary groups and schools is thought to be a factor in the relatively low level of vandalism, quite apart from its positive achievements.

I would like to say more about the achievements of other local authorities, but space does not permit. There is a lesson, for example, from the experience in London Boroughs and cities such as Leeds, of traffic management and children's play streets in residential areas. Several schemes which were brought in during the last 10 years have had to be scrapped or very much modified because of objections from residents, shop owners and road users. There is a limit to the redistribution which communities will tolerate.

Scottish local authorities have a good deal to tell us, too, about the important role of their local community councils (urban parish councils) in influencing environmental improvements. A special feature in Scotland is the work of the Scottish Development Agency, with its budget of £14 million for environmental improvements in Glasgow East Area Renewal, known as the GEAR project. It is early days for this as yet, but there will be important experience to be gained from its approach to co-operative working between local authorities, with their wide local responsibilities, and specific, task-orientated organisations such as the Agency. Then, within local government itself, the achievements of places like Greenock in improving dreary and socially deprived inter-war council estates have to be seen to be believed. They involve not merely rehabilitation, but, for example, detailed consideration of housing management policies, social work priorities for the Regional Council, standards of refuse collection and public cleansing.

Instructive, too, in addition to what I have already said about Liverpool, are the experiments in environmental care carried out there, based as they are on tidying up, making low-cost improvements and ensuring proper maintenance. And if one is looking for imaginative efforts to establish new landscape on a generous scale, with special help from schools by means of 'teacher packs' and 'bulb-ins', Warrington New Town, in Cheshire, is worth study. So are the efforts of the Great Manchester Council to improve the landscape and recreational attractions of its valleys – three country parks designated, a further three approved, three million trees planted and over £1m per annum spent on restoration and promotion. All this goes much further than their traditional work as planning authorities, though one must not play down the value of good and well balanced design guides and development briefs. But I must concentrate on what can be learnt from the examples I have been able to describe more fully.

My story has been necessarily factual so far, accounting for what has been done, and the context for that achievement. To what factors can success be attributed? What problems and shortcomings have emerged?

There are several elements which are common to each example. To start with, there has been strong political leadership, with a will to get things going to improve unusually bad environmental conditions – something of a crisis reaction. The environment, its qualities and management, has been made the subject of a programme in its own right, with a feeling for its totality; in some cases this has been able to extend right through to the treatment of walls, pavements, play spaces, etc and the quality of design involved. At the same time, the initiative taken by these councils has been organised across the board. Committees and departments have worked together, cutting red tape in common cause, and enthusing other agencies to re-tune their programmes to this end. Priorities have been determined at county level by techniques of assessment and evaluation, but at district level essentially by grass-roots opinion (which is as one would expect, having regard to the complexity of the issues, in strategic terms, and the strength of democratic links at the more local level). Local groups, including schools, have been closely involved with the work; people being regarded as an essential resource and a means of protection from vandalism. And, finally, there has been a go-getting approach to finance – cashing-in, literally, on the fairly generous grants that are available.

A success story indeed, but one that is not without difficulties. Strangely, finance has not always been regarded as the limiting factor, at least in the short term: 'Money has been the least of our worries – our difficulty has been to spend it.' Programmes seem to be dictated as much or more by shortages of manpower, design and implementation skills; by the time required for negotiations over land ownership or over financial contributions; by the time required to overcome inertia; and by the sheer numbers of people and organisations to be consulted in our two-tier system of local government. At all levels it is a labour-intensive business.

This relatively sanguine view is nevertheless essentially a short-term one. Time and time again, in talking to people who are doing the job, one senses their fears that, for all their efforts, the quality of the urban environment is deteriorating faster than they can improve it, and, in any case, the public are demanding higher standards all the time. Not that there is much evidence of precise standards being determined and used, other than in a strictly scientific sense, for example in pollution control; the state of the art is essentially pragmatic and opportunist. This is no bad thing, provided that the improvements work. Indeed, there is a case for more flexibility where standards are used extensively, such as in housing. In poorer neighbourhoods there is hardly the money available from owners and occupiers for repairs, and the take-up of improvement grants is consequently so low that area improvement has little impact. Have we been hoping for too much? Will we soon have to reconsider the relative priorities given to rehabilitation, on the one hand, and clearance and rebuilding, on the other? Issues of this kind will have a major impact on strategies and resources for environmental improvement in the future, since it is the really basic capital programmes that set the pace, a point which is well illustrated by the expenditure totals I have quoted for Bolton.

What conclusions can be drawn from all this for the street scene itself? I would summarise them as follows:

1 In those areas where the most determined efforts are being made towards environmental care and improvement, the *environment is regarded as a totality*, requiring a programme of action in its own right, closely related to other programmes, physical, social and economic, at strategic and local scales.

2 To get the best social return on scarce resources devoted to the environment, local authorities in these areas are co-operating and *concentrating their efforts* across the board in specific localities or on specific objectives. Small and low-cost improvements can thus combine with major capital projects such as housing rehabilitation to produce a relatively greater total effect. Without this they run the risk of being mere ad hoc cosmetic treatment.

3 In each case there is evidence of *strong political commitment* to environmental care and improvement, and an integrated organisation to follow it up, in-house and in conjunction with other agencies.

4 Whilst special studies are necessary for the determination of strategic priorities, local programmes can effectively be chosen pragmatically by expression of *grass-roots opinion*.

5 In each case there have been special arrangements for *involving local community groups, voluntary bodies and schools* in projects. This creates useful additional resources and a protective attitude towards the completed work.

6 Similarly, *the collaboration of private enterprise*, chambers of commerce, local industry, and of nationalised firms, has been a significant factor in several schemes.

7 It is essential to put aside *money for maintenance*.

8 Considerable extra resources can be created by making good use of government grants etc and of the *Job Creation Programme*.

9 The street scene is not only one of shopping streets and other eye-catching features. *Every street, wall, tree, back alley, and every bit of spare land matters.*

10 *Every town needs a strategy and programme for the improvement of its environmental quality, including visual delight through sensitive design of the kind advocated in this booklet. This outlook must pervade all the activities of its local authority.*

But when all is said and done, the fact remains that spending on the environment, even of the order illustrated in this article, is a mere drop in the ocean. To civilise the environment of our cities will be one of the prime social responsibilities of the rest of this century, and this will call for great financial sacrifices from better-off areas.

Meanwhile, we can make more progress with small-scale, low-cost improvements, the contribution of which to the whole environment will depend upon their relevance in a town's strategy for environmental care and improvement, and the appropriateness of the design in functional and aesthetic terms.

Selecting and siting street furniture

by Alfred A. Wood, DipArch, DipTP, FRIBA, FRTPI, FRSA, County Planner and Architect, West Midlands County Council.

ALFRED WOOD

DESIGN COUNCIL

ALFRED WOOD

Unusual items of street furniture act as visual punctuation marks in the street scene – some more delicate than others – but they can give rise to problems of co-ordination. Sensitivity to surroundings and careful project management are needed to produce harmonious results such as that achieved by the National Trust for Scotland at Corrieshalloch Gorge (below).

NATIONAL TRUST

'It's not what you do, it's the way that you do it' is probably the cardinal rule in furnishing our urban spaces. As necessary as household furniture, street furniture is almost always an after-thought in our urban surroundings. Only rarely (to judge by what we see about us) does it receive the same loving attention in selection and siting as would the furniture in our homes. Moreover, the fixtures are usually selected or specified by one group of people (rarely urban designers) but then installed by another. Urban spaces are our outdoor living-rooms, and the choice of furniture and especially the manner in which it is sited are major elements in the visual success or failure of our surroundings.

The development of street furniture from mileposts, railings, torch holders or street lamps to the many elements we see today provides a fascinating history of the use of materials and their effect on the urban scene. Footscrapers, bollards, clocks to mark the Relief of Mafeking perhaps, and eccentric street lamps are all basically utilitarian, but they also act as important visual punctuation marks in the street scene and often add richness and quality to spaces which might otherwise be bleak. The exuberance of Victorian cast ironwork or the fun and frolic of wrought-iron lamp brackets (seen by the passer-by as a sort of calligraphy against the sky), were and are pleasurable incidents in our everyday lives. The relative blankness of much current architecture in our streets emphasises the need to pay greater attention to enhancing their visual quality by careful selection and siting of street furniture.

Demands for more visual information for drivers, higher technical standards of illumination and so forth have led to the proliferation of street furniture of all kinds, some of it reasonably designed, but in total often ill considered in relation to the urban scene. Co-ordination is on the face of it relatively easy, but in fact it is a very difficult and complex business involving many agencies in central and local government and what we engagingly call the statutory undertakers. Rules for the siting and specification of trunk-road lighting by the Department of Transport have to be interpreted by local authorities; bus stop signs and bus shelters are erected by public transport operators but there are many other organisations involved in the process. If 'all the world's a stage and all the men and women merely players', the street furniture installation process is complicated by the fact that individual players have different scripts, and it is sometimes by no means certain that they are in the same play. Technical co-ordination is the hardest task in the world, as any observer of the British predilection for digging holes in the street will readily appreciate. No sooner has, say, a new stretch of paving been laid than some other group of people will dig it up and, after carrying out their doubtless vital task, will reinstate the footpath, but not quite in the same way as before.

But the difficulty of technical co-ordination is no reason for accepting visual mess in our towns, cities and countryside, and it is vital that local authorities exercise more vigilance in co-ordinating the activities of other furniture-erecting agencies, and considerably more sensitivity in carrying out their own operations.

Sensitivity to the surroundings in which street furniture is to be placed, and good aesthetic judgement in the choice of fitments, are essential qualities for those in charge of installation. But all too often there is a gap between those selecting street furniture and those whose task it is actually to site and install the articles. This gap is one of the reasons why we find those little rectangular blue parking signs (quite well designed in themselves) fixed to free-standing galvanised columns at the edge of the footpath instead of being fixed to a building: it is a nuisance to get approval from the building owner, and the soft option is to erect the separate post. Clearly in many local authorities the task of furnishing streets is considered to be a low-level job, and important aesthetic (and practical) considerations of this type are left to those who either have no sensitivity to the task in hand, or are given no authority to depart from methods laid down by superiors who, for ease of operation, lay down a standard solution for all occasions. A common example of insensitive rigidity is the use of full-sized 'no entry' signs in Conservation Areas. The Department of Transport is quite prepared to accept half-sized signs in such locations, under certain conditions, but the local authorities concerned rarely seem to seek this dispensation because it involves an administrative process and is frankly a nuisance.

There are at least five criteria to be considered in the selection process and these – suitability, scale, materials, fixings and numbers – all involve fitness for the task in hand. Most of them are very obvious indeed, but they are not always taken into account.

Fitness for purpose is clearly a crucial factor. Does the light fitting give the right illumination levels? Is the sign big enough or too large for its function? Is the seat comfortable as well as looking good?

Size and scale are not always considered sufficiently when street furniture is being selected: choosing a fitting from a catalogue can be dangerous and it may be sensible to try out different units on site, although this is obviously tiresome; time spent on reconnaissance is seldom wasted. Materials and their psychological impact are important. A concrete seat will certainly look heavier than a wooden one, even though its size may be similar. There are sizing implications too in the choice of materials: steel, concrete or timber posts for similar purposes have different dimensions which may affect their visual suitability. Maintenance is clearly a major factor and in Britain, regrettably, there is a need for fittings in certain areas to be vandal proof. Fixings and mountings need some consideration in that multiple use and flexibility can improve the versatility of individual units, reduce the range of supports needed and the numbers of supports. The design of fixings and mountings of signs and lamps should preferably be part of the overall visual concept. There will be places where fixing needs to be played down and where a sign can be applied to a wall, for example. Equally there will be cases in which the overall design of a family of fittings will rely very heavily on clean-cut fixings to increase visual attractiveness and versatility.

Choosing furniture, and particularly light fittings, for historic or sensitive areas is always a difficult process: there is the ever-present temptation to select units that have some echo of the past in the hope that they will fit into the general character of the street. This carries with it the danger of ghastly good taste, and it is generally better to choose simple, timeless

A sense of scale and the choice of appropriate materials are important selection criteria. The two seating areas (top and second from top) are both successful in this respect and in the sense of space they achieve, though they differ in style. Careful co-ordination and planning have transformed this bus stop in Upper Orwell Street, Ipswich.

25

Special items of street furniture, such as this drinking fountain in Albertslund, Denmark, (top) can add interest to a scheme, as can imaginatively placed lighting and planting such as that in Munich (centre) one of the earliest pedestrianised precincts, and appropriate architectural elements such as these lights in Chicago (below).

fittings that have no particular date stamped on them by their design. There may also be occasions when original lamp brackets or posts may be used with the addition of new lanterns. Compatibility of scale, materials and shape are obvious factors to take into account in these circumstances, as well as the need for proper performance. Familiarity is also an important element in selection: a litter bin which looks like a litter bin is more likely to be used than some of the overdesigned examples found in many manufacturers' catalogues.

Consideration for the users of street furniture needs to be emphasised too. In particular, the requirements of the disabled, and especially the blind, tend to be overlooked. In the past street nameplates, for example, were often made of cast iron with raised letters and in suburban areas at least were at heights within people's reach. Apart from the fact that such nameplates usually employed stylish fat-face typefaces and were elegant in their own right, they were extremely useful for the blind: it would surely be possible, using cast aluminium or a suitable plastics material, to provide modern versions which would be at once attractive and useful.

There has been a generally welcome trend recently towards fewer light fittings, particularly with high-mast road lighting, but although in some cases one big one may be better than four little ones this is not always the case. In small-scale areas it may well be easier to handle the visual impact of several smaller units and, provided that function is not impaired, grouping may also be considered. Light fittings can give cohesion to a street if handled well: equally, insensitive siting can drive a visual hole through an otherwise pleasant space.

Siting is at least as difficult, and certainly more complex, than the process of selection. Performance criteria for signs are laid down by the Department of the Environment and very sensibly illustrated in *Circular 7/75*. This publication suggests a range of solutions to sizing and siting problems that totally belies the stereotyped and unimaginative examples that we actually find in our streets. There is obviously a need for street furniture selectors and installers, not only to study and understand the regulations covering the use of signs and fittings, but more specifically fully to appreciate the accompanying advice which allows for intelligent interpretation of the use of criteria and can lead to applications with that spark of creativity which produces schemes in harmony with the surroundings.

Street furniture can influence the sense of place, particularly as the pedestrian perceives it, and it is crucial that eye level should play a proper part in siting. Eye level largely determines the basis of scale in a street and it is vital that the impact of furniture should be related to the needs of the space as seen by people who use it.

A straw poll in any town would undoubtedly reveal a demand for more seating in many areas – and what is more for seating that is comfortable. Although backless seats look well, most people like backrests and armrests; there is a great deal to be said for individual chairs, as used in the large pedestrian street system in central Munich. Seating areas should generally be protected from main pedestrian routes and they should cater both for those who like sun and for those who prefer shade. They must also allow the occupants to indulge in one of the favourite human activities, watching the passing crowd; homo sapiens likes to regard his own kind and finds it particularly agreeable if his seat is slightly above the general level of the surrounding area. Sensible and sensitive planting can also add greatly to the sense of relaxation, and can help to create that oasis feeling so important in town centres. It is important for seating to be arranged, not with municipal order in mind so much as with appreciation of how people will enjoy

 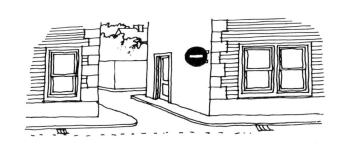

 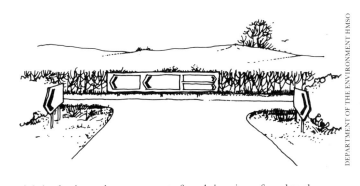

DEPARTMENT OF THE ENVIRONMENT HMSO

Badly placed signs are often the result of unintelligent interpretation of regulations, as these Department of the Environment examples show. (Top left and right) a badly placed sign clutters the street and blocks the view, and a sign sited against a house silhouette may be preferable. (Centre left and right) one wall-mounted no entry sign is preferable to two signs that block the pavement. (Bottom left and right) a horizontal arrangement of road signs is preferred to the complicated and obtrusive one.

(Below) planting, lighting, seating, display and surface treatment all play a part in successful pedestrianisation schemes, and all need to be properly related one to another by careful planning and installation.

J. W. TOMKINS, WEST MIDLANDS COUNTY COUNCIL.

The Bahnhofstrasse in Zurich (above left) provides an example of the use of a family of street furniture based on the same dimensional grid as the paving. Contrast this meticulous approach with the horrific tangle of services shown below (below left). Skidmore, Owings and Merrill used plain globe light fittings in the Carlton Centre in Johannesburg (above centre). This is modern city jewellery, which offsets what might otherwise be a rather stark scheme. The splendid water feature in Oldenburg (above right).

provides a spectacular foreground to the painstakingly renovated surroundings. Even with good materials it is possible to forget the needs of users. The surface in Fitzroy Square in London (bottom left) deters pedestrians as well as cyclists because the gutters are too wide. The pedestrian area in Mildenhall (below right) provides a sense of space but is practical as well.

the location. A recently 'improved' civic space in a major Midlands city has most of the seats facing north to the Town Hall when the interesting (and sunny) prospect is in exactly the opposite direction.

Street furniture siting can be defensive, too. In areas that are predominantly traffic free, but used occasionally by buses or trucks, street furniture can be used to protect the pedestrian from unexpected traffic. The system of paving must also be considered as part of the siting process, especially in pedestrian areas. Suitably selected materials can be the unifying matrix that binds the separate elements of furniture into a cohesive whole. Paving materials can also be used to direct any vehicles which occasionally have to use an otherwise traffic-free area, thus helping to emphasise those zones in which the pedestrian should dominate and differentiating them from roads where traffic should be relatively untramelled.

As with seating, there is a real need to try to understand human behaviour when siting street furniture, particularly litter bins. These are a constant source of argument: one school of thought has it that litter bins, especially when full (they always seem to be full) *cause* unsightly litter rather than curing the problems created by living in what is by common consent the biggest litter-creating nation on earth. Indeed, some county councils have, with some success, removed litter bins from trunk road lay-bys on the basis that their absence en-courages people to take rubbish home. In urban surroundings, however, litter bins seem to be effective when sited in zones of slow movement of pedestrians. Shopping streets, sitting areas, car parks and bus stops are probably the most suitable places. If litter bins are merely placed in arbitrary positions on a pedestrian route they tend to encourage the ill aimed throw which deposits the rubbish on the pavement. The obvious rule is therefore to site bins close to the point of litter production in positions where they can be integrated with other elements of street furniture and where they can be easily emptied.

Lighting is probably the most difficult single element in street furniture selection and siting. Although there is ostensibly a great deal of choice, it is more apparent than real, especially in the case of Group B lighting which does not offer the alternatives required for use in the most sensitive areas where people and vehicles must co-exist. High-mast lighting techniques have improved, as have Group A designs, and it should be possible to select and site satisfactorily from the range available. In the smaller-scale locations requiring Group B fittings, however, lack of choice may require custom-made fittings to suit the ambience of the area: this does not necessarily imply great additional expense.

There have been a number of successful lighting schemes produced for the new role of pedestrianised streets, but these are outweighed by unsuccessful schemes which fail to exploit the potential of the situation. The scale of the lighting system, the need to highlight street furniture hazards for the pedestrian, and the opportunities that exist to emphasise the architectural qualities of the street both above and below shop fascias are all important factors. The appearance of the fittings in daylight as well as at night, and neat fixings, preferably to buildings, are also crucial points. It may well be possible to use floodlight schemes for selected buildings in the street scene in such a manner as to replace conventional lighting in some sectors. In areas where vehicles and pedestrians must co-exist closely, balustrade lighting and lighting bollards could be used more extensively without confusing the motorist. A relatively inexpensive way of introducing delight and magic into our

(Below left) this scheme in Totnes, Devon, is perhaps rather bleak and rigid at present, but will improve as the trees grow. It can be compared with the rather more fluid treatment of the street corner in Abingdon, Oxfordshire (below right).

towns, lighting must be considered carefully as one of the basic elements of street furniture.

The success of urban spaces is usually dependent on the relationship between the scale of the area and man. The crucial factor here is to select the street furnishings carefully to emphasise the new human-scale role of the pedestrianised street. Paving materials, usually the simpler the better, need to relate to buildings and to people. Elements to be used in the open air should usually be a little larger than the same elements employed internally: outside steps should generally, for example, be about 200mm in rise.

Fitness for purpose again must be a prime factor and there is usually a great deal to be said for simplicity. Clearly it is often sensible to recover and use old granite setts and the like. The aim should be to enhance and complement existing structures rather than to display excessive visual virtuosity, which can sometimes detract from the existing scene. The homespun has a place in our surroundings and care should be taken not to over-dress the locality. Natural colour in materials is generally more successful than highly coloured artificial alternatives, and there is no substitute for quality.

Although they are one of the simplest and most effective townscape devices, changes in level are often overlooked when pedestrian streets are created. Stairs, platforms, terraces and ramps enable people to have a different view of the scene and allow them a more pleasurable kinetic sensation. Attention must be given to access, however, particularly for the disabled and for pram pushers. There should always be an alternative, easy route when changes of level are employed.

As in most other elements, simplicity is usually the most effective discipline in planting schemes, particularly as regards the design of shrub boxes, flower pots and the like. Leafy plants are usually more successful than flowers; greenery tends to complement the profusion of colour which is usually present in shop window displays and in people's clothes. If vandalism takes place it is usually best to replace the missing plants at once and not to publicise the damage. Frequent attention may, however, be necessary to remove rubbish from shrub boxes.

Water features can be effective in warm climates, but tend to be over-used and rather out of place in chilly and wet northern latitudes. If employed, movement and the pleasing sound of falling water are clearly valuable elements in the urban scene, and moving water tends to be relatively self-cleansing. It may seem obvious to point out that water features should be sited where fountains and spray are not affected by cross-winds and cannot therefore drench the passer-by, but it is surprising how often this is overlooked.

When traffic is removed from a street, litter that was formerly swept into the gutters by passing vehicles becomes a very obvious element in the scene. It is therefore necessary to provide for more frequent street sweeping and cleansing.

It is clearly essential to allow proper access for fire engines, the police, ambulances, building contractors and so forth. Normally this can be done by providing sufficient width (usually 3m minimum) between items of furniture, by ensuring that paving strength is adequate for the weight of vehicles, and by arranging that there are alternatives to steps where changes of level take place.

Many people obtain great satisfaction from noticing, albeit only half consciously, the details they see in everyday journeys round their towns and cities. Although we live in a period which is in many ways visually impoverished, there are nevertheless signs of improvement in street furniture design and in its application. One of the more hopeful elements has been the real improvement in the quality of thought and advice issuing from departments of state, particularly the Department of Transport and the Department of the Environment. There is now little excuse for their agents, the local authorities and the statutory undertakers, to make a mess of our surroundings by ill-considered application of street furniture. The components are there, flexibility of application is catered for; all we require is sensitivity in the selection and siting of street furniture to enhance the urban scene.

Traditional materials used in a stylish way in Richmond, Surrey (above left) with well integrated seating, but the litter basket is poorly sited, right in the middle of the view. Water in combination with natural and man-made materials (above right) provides a visually coherent and interesting space in Stuttgart's Schlossgarten.

Texture and pattern are important in breaking up what could otherwise be bland and uninteresting surfaces (left and below left). The difference between simply removing traffic and actively promoting an area for pedestrian use is graphically shown (below) in these two sketches of a town market before and after a thorough and sensitive application of street furniture.

Streets in historic areas

by Reginald Hyne, DiPArch, DipSP, FRIBA, Principal of Edgington, Spink & Hyne, Windsor, Chairman, Berkshire Society of Architects 1975–77 and Consultant to the Royal Borough of Windsor and Maidenhead for Windsor Conservation Area.

Thanks largely to the 'outrage' movement of the mid 1950s and the birth of the Civic Trust in 1957, the value of historic areas as part of our unfolding history has been recognised. The 'Facelift' schemes of the Civic Trust and their invention of Conservation Areas in 1967 has ensured that everyone from the junior school desk to the Government benches appreciates our architectural heritage.

The future of old places is at last assured. A veritable army of amenity societies up and down Great Britain is making sure that not only the Winchesters of this world are protected, but also the modest Victorian streets in Watford or Wapping. Fortunately, in this the amenity societies have the whole-hearted support of most planning officers and councillors.

Originally, historic areas accommodated almost nothing in the way of 'street furniture'. The whole street served as a litter bin, and any lighting was provided by a flambeau of pitched rope: beware of the belief that converted gas lamps are always right in old streets! Hot, dry areas provided cool seats and sparkling fountains and great characters were celebrated in dramatic sculptures. Cold, wet places supplied cast-iron coal chutes underfoot, boot scrapers at the front door, and every-where solid practical drinking troughs for man's best friends – dogs and horses.

Historic areas now demand the paraphernalia of street furniture required by any modern area; indeed more so. The invading admirers arrive by the plane load from far-flung corners of the world. In towns like Windsor the flood of sight-seers is almost as great in winter as in summer. The local authorities and boards of every description have to direct and instruct them; protect and make safe their various ways; lighten their darkness and discreetly accept their refuse and dispose of it efficiently. Tourists bring untold pressures on his-toric places which have not been designed to accommodate either them or the street furniture they, and we, now need.

How then is the problem to be tackled? To begin with, can some of the problems which give rise to the need for street furniture be reduced or eliminated?

Some street furniture problems could be solved more readily merely by sensible legislation. Historic areas, it is true, are granted some privileges over others, but what is visually less obtrusive for conservation areas would also be a benefit for others. Yellow lines can be 25 per cent narrower and a little less yellow in a conservation area, but their accompanying signs and posts are all part of the visually disturbing street clutter. Rational legislation could eliminate them altogether and a positive rather than a negative method of indicating 'No Park-ing' minimises the need for signs. The riverside pedestrian area at Windsor displays a sign: 'Restricted zone except for load-ing'. Here the police can enforce no waiting or parking without the need for yellow lines.

Choosing street furniture

Each historic area is unique and must be considered on its merit. What is good for one might be quite unsuitable for another, but if an area is to 'live' changes must be accepted in the furnishings of the street as readily as changes to the sur-rounding buildings.

It hasn't helped the task of the co-ordinating designer that manufacturers of the many components have paid no attention to the special needs of historic areas. Lighting manufacturers make all sorts of reproduction gas lamps, but imitations of any sort are unlikely to be satisfactory. Rooting around antique markets for old cast-away gas lamps may be a solution for a very special place, but generally modern needs of lighting, just

as modern needs of litter collection, need modern solutions.

Before furniture is chosen for any area a survey must be made; in an historic area, a careful survey is of paramount importance. There is no better way of becoming familiar with a place than by looking at, and noting on a plan, every item of impedimenta – from yellow lines and cobbles to television aerials. It is worth noting all the historic hardware, the cast-iron coal chute covers, boot scrapers and manhole covers: some might be found with attractive hardwood inlays. Changes of level, ramps, steps, railings and handrails are all important characteristics to be noted and later exploited.

Getting a feel for the place in this way will help enormously in making the right choice for new furniture. For example, an area generously endowed with iron railings might call for outdoor seating and litter bins based on steel frame and slatted wood designs rather than concrete.

It is difficult to generalise, but while it would not be sensible to retain a lamp standard which for some reason can never again shed a glimmer of light, it would be folly to destroy a useless, but intrinsically interesting object like an ornamented cast-iron fire hydrant. Similarly, it would be lamentable to remove a bronze horse trough: the space it occupies can be justified on the grounds that it is a museum piece; a container of sparkling water; or perhaps a box for plant material.

Road surfaces

Unlike Continental countries, Holland in particular, we have not managed to do without tarmac on our road surfaces. This relatively modern invention does nothing for historic streets. It is a destroyer of spaces and surfaces and wherever possible should be removed. This is especially important where it has cheaply replaced stone pavement slabs.

Wherever possible original paving for roads and pavements should be reinstated. If this is not possible, they should be re-surfaced with locally reclaimed materials; in this way instant maturity is achieved and this is worth while in many instances. Alternatively, a choice can be made from the excellent range of naturally coloured concrete examples which are available as plain paviours for brick-like herringbone arrangements or interlocking patterns; there is also a range of good quality paving bricks. The emphasis in an historic area should always be on quality whatever the material.

Surfaces of concrete setts are no more expensive to provide and lay than tarmac: they are excellent wherever slow speeds are desired; they are especially suitable for heavy loads; and no maintenance is required. An additional advantage is that roads can be invisibly repaired following any sub-surface excavations.

The raising of road surfaces to pavement level is fairly common in newly pedestrianised streets. In this way emphasis is given to the pedestrian character of the space and freedom of movement is allowed over the whole surface. However, this is not necessarily advisable in a narrow street when limited access is permitted for vehicles unloading; although the un-broken surface broadens the appearance of the street the orig-inal upstanding kerb serves to keep vehicles a safe distance from buildings, and this is important where there are project-ing upper storeys, shop blinds or hanging signs. Cobbled sur-faces can include 'wheeler' stone tracks as a guide to vehicles.

Lighting

Electricity for street lighting is essentially a twentieth-century invention and in most instances it is logical and sensible to

(Below and top right) the pedestrianisation scheme for Corn Street in Bristol makes use of a simply laid and appropriate stone surface and a minimum of additional street furniture. What items there are reinforce and emphasise the architecture. Some areas will need more lighting than this, however. (Bottom right) modern street furniture and surfaces equally can complement existing features, like these period railings at Windsor.

CITY OF BRISTOL.

CITY OF BRISTOL.

CITY OF BRISTOL.

REGINALD HYNE.

accept this fact and take every advantage of modern lighting technology to enhance the night-time scene.

There are three categories of lighting: general, amenity and decorative. General lighting can be provided at high level by wall-mounted lamps or lamps on posts; amenity lighting by medium-height standards and wall mountings, and at a lower level in bollards and balustrades on ramps and steps. Decorative lighting includes the floodlighting of key buildings, sculptures, monuments and fountains, also the lighting of planted areas and trees. Bollard lighting and other low-level forms which are effective only over a limited area can draw attention to special pedestrian areas and car parking spaces.

All these sources of possible lighting should be considered, and they should be exploited where suitable opportunities exist. An experienced lighting engineer can work miracles with the appearance of an area at night when a co-ordinated scheme is appropriate.

In an historic place with informal street patterns and diverse building styles, wall-mounted fittings are likely to be the most suitable. The very essence of the choice of a modern lighting fitting is that it should be self effacing; when not shedding light is should be unobserved.

Retaining and converting old lamps, replacing those missing and adding others to raise the level of illumination is a perfectly legitimate and justifiable objective where the quality and character of the area would be degraded by introducing sleek, modern tubes.

At all costs a regimented pattern of uniform heights and intervals should be avoided; an illuminated tunnel is quite the last thing one wants.

Woodstock and Burford in Oxfordshire provide excellent examples of the use of wall-mounted fittings. In these predominantly stone towns the general lighting is from simple box-like fittings tucked high under the eaves. The finish and colour are neutral and in daylight one must look hard at the buildings to spot them.

The formal setting presented by Georgian or Victorian terraces presents a particular problem, as wall-mounted lights could spoil such an area. Traditionally these streets might have had gas lamps on cast-iron standards or even early electric lamp standards. Gas lanterns were supported from beneath and incorporated cross-bar rests; electric lamps were more often suspended with a mechanical lowering device for maintenance. These cast-iron standards were often richly moulded and ornamented.

Where it is not possible to connect up the gas supply – and usually it is not – good examples of gas lamps can be converted to electricity. If the old lamp posts cannot be adapted to accommodate the new lighting cables, they can be connected to separate feeder pillars unobtrusively sited and specially designed to contain the switch gear. The old Westminster City Council adopted this solution for Queen Anne's Gate.

Litter bins

The selection of suitable litter bin designs from standard ranges is very difficult and the technical services departments of all district authorities administering historic areas meet with the same problems. Unfortunately there seems to be no simple townscape equivalent of the bin for rural picnic places – often a cheap sturdy frame with plastic bag and flip-up lid concealed in a screen of slender tree trunks.

The chosen material should harmonise with local building materials. Reconstructed stone or easily cleaned fine exposed aggregate concrete is an obvious choice where there are stone and brick, or stone buildings. A revival of terracotta might be worth an experiment in brick-built environments. Many of the sheet metal and slatted timber designs can look very well in certain situations, for instance next to planted areas or related to slatted seats. A disadvantage in busy places is that they are easily damaged.

Seats

Traditionally, seats lined our seaside promenades and town parks. With the exclusion of traffic from ancient streets to form pedestrian precincts, many more opportunities are created for their use.

As with lamp posts, original examples should be retained and refurbished for re-use, or transplanted if no longer suitable where found. Victorian piers have splendidly comfortable examples which should be cherished; some modern ones reflect this spirit and look well in association with other ironwork.

Solid looking seats with supports of precast concrete with exposed aggregate finish, combining hardwood slats or planks look well in almost any historic area – especially where stone predominates. Special seats, looking more like part of the townscape than imported ready-made examples, can be very simply made up from a plank of wood or timber slats set into a purpose-built stone or brick wall.

Specials built to suit a particular location can obviously combine with many other essential items of street furniture, from bins to bus shelters, thus simplifying the overall problem of co-ordination. Trees can be protected by seats built round their bases.

Bollards

Bollards were almost the first arrivals on the street scene. They came in stone and cast iron and were used to prevent the passage of wheeled vehicles or to protect the bases of buildings, especially at corners and at the jambs of openings, where they were placed at an angle leaning towards the building. They can still fulfil this traditional protective function, both for pedestrians and for buildings.

Beautiful cast-iron bollards exist in many historic areas; none should ever be discarded: when no longer functional they should be transplanted to useful locations. Some bollards are up-turned cannons, others were cast in imitation; the ornate bases of lamp posts were also used. All the cast-iron examples are of historic interest; sometimes they were specially cast for a particular location, with a monogram and date. In some of the old London boroughs those traditionally in use are sturdy but slender truncated pyramids with horizontal ribbing; they are models of functional simplicity. Additional replica castings have been made to supplement the existing examples in historic GLC areas; in special circumstances, this possibility should always be borne in mind.

Plain concrete bollards lacking any detail are not appropriate for historic areas, but there are some standard examples of simple designs in good quality finishes which will fit very comfortably into such places.

Bus shelters

Whenever possible, bus shelters should be purpose built in harmonious materials; integrated with existing walls or buildings, they are immediately absorbed into the fabric of the area. Alternatively, they should be designed as part of a group of other essential kiosks or seats, with as few bits and pieces standing about and obstructing already narrow pavements as

This handsomely restored fountain in Kingston upon Hull is lit strategically by concealed floodlights let into the kerb. This sort of detail design is particularly important in historic areas, as these three examples from Chester show. New cast-iron lamps (below left) were made specially with a period flavour, as were the hardwood bollards (below centre). The cast-iron bollards (below right) match their cobbled surroundings perfectly. The degree to which historic areas require furnishing should always be considered. The resurfaced Stonegate area of York (bottom) is a good example of a site in which extra street furniture would probably be superfluous.

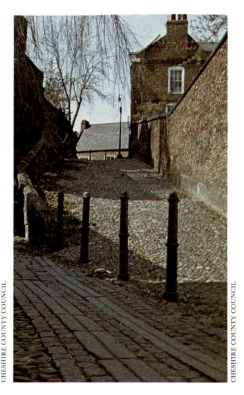

possible. Bus shelters which incorporate advertising panels are unlikely to be suitable for this sort of area.

In places where there is no alternative to standing a bus shelter on a pavement, it should be as transparent as possible to make it less obtrusive. Any type with solid corrugated panels should not be chosen. In all cases the addition of a bus stop pole should be avoided; any necessary information should be incorporated into the design of the shelter.

Display and advertising fittings

So far as is commercially possible, display and advertising fittings should not be used in historic areas. However, a group of trades people tucked away in a corner may need to announce their presence, and an appropriate sign for them can usually be combined on a display unit with directions to public lavatories or a car park.

Advertising of every description should be controlled to the fullest extent of local authority powers. Over-sized fascia boards, aggressively large lettering and illuminated advertisement signs should be avoided in architecturally sensitive areas. Traditional three-dimensional hanging signs which exist should be cherished. Where new advertising signs are commercially imperative, new three-dimensional signs without display lettering could be considered.

Signs

Signs of every description tend to pop up like mushrooms; in historic areas there should be as few as possible. Shiny slabs of colourful stove enamelling are difficult to absorb, when all that was necessary in the past were street names, and these were attractive castings with raised letters.

Historic signs of good quality and which are still useful should be retained. New street name signs can still be made in traditional ways where this seems appropriate, however modern signs with clear, simple lettering can also be used.

The back of a road sign can give as much offence as the front – not all are double sided; such signs should be set against a background of planting or on a wall without supporting poles.

Route signs placed on historic buildings can be visually disastrous and crude lane markings are equally disruptive. Highway authorities should endeavour to eliminate signs and supporting poles of every kind.

Telephone kiosks

Telephone kiosks can be very unpleasant to use and are frequently out of order as a result of vandalism; it is a pity we can't manage without them as seems to be the case on the Continent. There, public telephones are found in supervised places like bars and restaurants, thus killing two birds with one stone – they are not damaged by vandals and they are not a blot on the townscape.

The current kiosk design fits fairly well into most areas, provided they are not ranged side by side like battery hen boxes. Used singly and sited unobtrusively or grouped with other elements, they are satisfactory, particularly if they are painted in a greyish colour, as in the Cotswolds. The distinctive red, if necessary, could be reserved for a small panel at the top. If more than one telephone is required in a sensitive area, a purpose-built structure divided into cubicles and linked with other buildings is likely to be less intrusive.

Pillar boxes

Pillar boxes present no problems at all when they are built in, and Victorian ones are still used successfully where demand is

not great. However, where possible the Post Office likes to keep up to date with Royal monograms; this can sometimes mean that a Victorian pillar box, beloved of local users, is in danger of being swept away, especially if the mouth is particularly small. Modern boxes are designed to make collection easier, but in certain cases a distinctive old box can be retained.

Window boxes and shutters

Nothing detracts from the appearance of a building more than empty window boxes. But those which are meticulously planted and kept fresh and full can make buildings more cheerful and inviting. However, window boxes must be purpose designed to suit the window; when placed on the top of the sill they can destroy the interest of the glazing. The indiscriminate use of standard plastics or rustic types should be discouraged. Window boxes should not be used on timber-framed buildings because constant watering can cause damage if it enters haircracks in the rendering.

Window shutters which are original and form part of the design of the building should be retained at all cost. Fake shutters nailed to the wall should be avoided.

Railings and balustrades

Many delightful balustrades disappeared during the early days of the Second World War in a welter of local authority activity; iron gates and railings, saucepans and frying pans were collected and melted down to make guns and aircraft.

Where possible, damaged or missing railings should be replaced; new castings can be made to match the old ones, using fragments or photographs for reference. Local authority grants may be given to help with the cost.

Where modern railings are needed to protect pedestrians, something straightforward, bold and sturdy should be chosen. Materials to be avoided include concrete in almost any standard mass-produced form, angle iron and chain link. Aluminium with a suitable finish, iron, steel and timber are all possibilities. A simple steel tube, bent to form both post and handrail, might be a sufficient barrier in some places, in others a straightforward balustrade in a rhythmic vertical pattern made in bold sturdy metalwork would look right.

Trees

It is sometimes difficult to introduce trees into an area not originally designed with them in mind. The removal of traffic from squares and streets should provide new opportunities for planting trees unless they are very narrow. In addition to their value as things of natural beauty in their own right and in the pleasure they bring into the urban scene as a reminder of the passing seasons, trees can ease immeasurably the difficult task of uniting other more difficult items of furniture; for instance they can dominate a telephone kiosk or traffic sign.

An intrusive building or an untamable fascia board as seen from a particularly important viewpoint can be screened, at least partially, by the planting of a group of trees. In a narrow street an opportunity for the tree planting might occur where one building is set back, or where there is a garden or courtyard wall, rather than a building. Here a tree that grows behind a wall and spreads over the top into the street can bring a welcome hint of nature into the perspective of a man-made urban scene. In all cases trees must be protected from damage from vehicles, either by kerbs, containing walls, or by surrounding seats.

Display advertising for nearby shops close to Windsor Bridge (right) has been sensitively handled and is a welcome addition to the street scene. The road sign in Newbury (below left) is much less attractively sited and in fact obscures part of the front of a listed building. One of its supports is redundant and blocks the footpath and the whole sign would be better placed on the corner of the building. Paving in Durham (below right) has been carefully planned and installed to fit in with its historic surroundings, with provision for access by vehicles when necessary.

The rationalisation and improvement of West Wemyss, Fife,
(below) has been carried out in a sympathetic way, using modern
designs and materials.

Outdoor lighting in towns

by Donald Insall, FSA, FRIBA, FRTPI, DipSP, Principal of Donald W. Insall and Associates, London.

Lighting towns is both an art and a science, with much more to it than merely choosing attractive lamp-standards and calculating suitable spacing for them. And indeed, in this country where we all spend so much time by artificial light, the benefits of a good and well designed installation are surely worth all the effort, thought and experiment they entail.

The purpose of lighting is simply to define and describe the forms of things which would otherwise be in darkness. Expanding from this, lighting may be intended to help people to move around after dark, either on foot or in vehicles, by revealing the buildings and objects in the environment, for everyone's safety. Its purpose may be partly to give us pleasure, by describing and explaining the form of what we see. And by its mood and colour, lighting can underline and influence our emotional reaction to every night scene.

It is worth considering some basic points about lighting and optics. The first one to remember is that light from a lamp has no effect until it falls upon a visible surface which reflects it back to the eye of an observer. For this reason, a lamp on a pole can by itself be stark and meaningless. True, its very existence will signify some message; but light cannot possibly help anything to be seen until it falls on a reflecting surface, be it a wall or a road, a building or a tree. Yet we are all familiar with the bleak vapidity of random lamp-bulbs suspended high against the sky, with nothing to shine upon or reveal.

The next significant point in lighting design is that the superb sensitivity of the human eye enables it to deal with an incredible range of brightness, from the faintest star in the heavens to blazing direct sunlight bouncing off a desert or shimmering on a brilliant and sandy beach. To deal with this extreme range, first the iris of the eye reacts immediately to the most brilliant light-source in sight, selecting for itself a range of acceptable brightnesses, like the iris in a camera lens. Then, more slowly, the optic nerve adapts itself to the required subject range.

Once the range of perceivable lighting is established by the eye, the inner brain takes command. As every window-dresser and every photographer knows, 'the eye follows the light', and it is to the brightest points that our attention is first called. But shade (the relative absence of light) and shadow (the unlit region shielded from light by an object) are as important in describing form as light itself; for the two are interdependent and complement each other. Shape is shown by darkness as well as by light.

Because of these two factors, lighting design becomes a matter simply of handling and presenting a range of reflecting surfaces against the context of the brightest visible light source. If the source itself can be screened, the eye can expand the selected range of the other brightnesses it can perceive. Thus 'glare' from any source disastrously limits our ability to see and apprehend subtler reflecting surfaces around it. A single extra glaring light will in fact immediately reduce the visibility of everything but itself.

The main technical components of lighting are its intensity and its colour (both in impression, and in detailed composition). Tungsten lighting is both warm in colour and random in composition, but modern gas-discharge lamps on the other hand are often very limited in wavelength. Low-pressure sodium lighting, for example, emits only orange light; and since no green light is emitted, green foliage and grass receive nothing they can reflect, and as a result can only look almost black. These lamps are economical and efficient, but can appear somewhat bleak. This is partly because the source itself is usually large, and glows at a fairly low intensity. On the other hand, the concentrated beams of light from a point

Outdoor lighting has a decorative role as well as a practical one in many cases, as these examples from (top) Göteborg, Sweden, (centre) Warrington and (bottom) the Place Carnot, Lyons, show. But the daytime effect of these 'lollipop' fittings can be very bleak, and great care is needed with lamps seen against the sky and without surfaces to shine upon.

source, such as a spotlamp or car headlamp, are more glaring if not shielded or very carefully directed, and are more strongly directional and descriptive. A multiplicity of low-brightness, large light sources are therefore flattening and shadowless in effect, whereas spotlighting, although glaring, reveals the details and texture of what it lights. The lighting engineer will be instinctively conscious of and knowledgeable about these differences, but he may forget to explain or predict the various effects they will create.

While outdoor lighting is the art of selecting and distributing light sources in such a way that surfaces are well illuminated and exposed, in practice the principles of street lighting have become strongly codified by traffic regulations. The real challenge is still to understand what we are trying to achieve. Do we, for example, really want each route to be lit at the same brilliance? And would it be better for lighting along any route to build up gradually to a maximum and then taper off? If the light must change colour, can it signal something useful? And what about the town we are lighting? Since 'the eye goes to the light', have we positioned our lamps so that they illuminate what we would most like to see? For example, certain key buildings may be the special pride of a town; their good lighting becomes a strong element in the regular pattern of light at night – in the 'message' and image of the city. And if these buildings are floodlit, the brightness of their lighting has a strong relationship with all the other outdoor lights, whose visibility and significance this brighter light will quickly overpower.

Next comes the pattern of light sources themselves, and the way in which they are distributed. This has a powerful impact, as can be seen clearly from the air at night. Lines of light describe for us the hierarchy of routes, but the way they are scattered may in practice confuse instead of clarifying. A bridge may look attractive set with marching clusters of lights reflected in a river, but its effect after dark can be meaningless if its lamps are repositioned, alternating to left and right pavements, without any telling rhythm or order. The linear effect of fluorescent tubes especially is very marked, and can explain the direction of a road or create the impression of a chaotic and angular state of confusion.

The science of street lighting for traffic safety owes much to reflection and to shadow. Traffic lighting installations are theoretically designed so that light will be bounced off the road, half way between each successive lamp and the approaching car. So the surface ahead of the motorist as he drives along a road will be a succession of reflected pools of light against which any obstacle or pedestrian stands out in a dark shadow. There is an innate contradiction between this and the use of car headlamps in towns, since although these enable the pedestrian to see a car more quickly and warn him of its approach, they also cancel out for the motorist the effect of seeing pedestrians silhouetted as black objects against these horizontal patches of reflected light. Some clear thinking is needed to sort this one out.

The siting of lampposts, brackets and impedimenta is a difficult and sometimes thankless task, particularly in sensitive and historic areas. In general, simplicity pays – metal should look like metal, and concrete like concrete (I once identified some wooden lampposts in Boston, USA, greatly to the astonishment and delight of local people). But posts are a nuisance. Often, in narrower streets, the best answer has been to use wall brackets; and these can be very tidy and acceptable. Care is then needed, however, in the design of the lighting unit itself, for unless light is cast back onto the wall from which such a lamp is suspended, there will be a glaring spot of light shining from darkness. Alternatively if such a light is very near its wall and too bright, the street surface will by contrast look unlit.

Questions of legal rights of support, the run of necessary wiring and avoiding too much light cast into windows will also call for ingenuity and negotiation. Before recommending suitable units, the lighting engineer will of course need to know what maintenance and cleaning any installation will receive, the hours during which it will be used, and what switching systems are preferred.

Then again, what will be the daytime appearance of the lamps? In many towns and cities, history has provided superbly decorative lamp-standards, peculiar to the traditions of a place. The 'dolphin' standards along London's Embankment, and the great lamp-standards in Trafalgar Square come immediately to mind. The paired lamps of Edinburgh's stately squares, growing from railings and steps, define at one stroke both the public square and each private entrance.

Each place, after all, has its special character which it should surely be our task and pleasure to reinforce. The outburst of carriage lamps which appears in any newly gentrified quarter often destroys the whole essence of a neighbourhood. Carriage lamps are best on carriages, and a town should look itself. A port should look like a port, and nautical gear is appropriate in its place, but it can look silly inland. Lamps like giant plastic saucers on sticks may be right for a motorway but are wrong in a village. Colour also matters: gay seaside or spa colours may have their place, or metal may look best in black; the important thing is to think about it before the brush goes into the paint-pot, for then it will be too late.

Very old lamps, especially, are a ticklish problem, but they are also an opportunity. Old gas lamps still survive in some towns and are a part of their spirit. There is no point in pulling them down needlessly; and a less obvious but equally disastrous attempt at progress can be to electrify and modernise them, and even to glaze them with diffused glass. By day the lanterns may look much the same, but the night effect is utterly different, and may be far inferior. An even unhappier fate awaits the decent old lamppost which is lopped and topped and given an entirely unsuitable new lantern, perhaps with a light source nobody would have chosen for its particular shape or height. Another mistake is to install a blinding new floodlight within the ambience of a perfectly-balanced existing set of street lamps.

Lighting is indeed an art, and the best way to be sure is to try out an effect before installing it permanently. We could with enormous advantage experiment with lighting far more than we do, for temporary installations can help to check the effects before money is wasted in permanent mistakes. Shop displays and private lighting (although excluded from any consideration by the Codes of Practice) do for example contribute importantly to the overall effect of lighting in any city at night, but are difficult to allow for on paper.

So the successful design of an outdoor lighting installation calls for expert technical knowledge, but also for a special awareness of the qualities of a place. It requires a flexibility of approach, and a willingness to experiment or try alternative solutions, knowing what we seek to achieve. Only then can the light of reason shine through, in the reason for the light.

Norwich designed and produced their own street light, shown here (top left and left) in wall and post-mounted installations. These can be contrasted with the outmoded and ugly installation (top centre) of the type that can still be found around Britain. Lighting narrow alleys and passages can be a problem. This example on a modern housing estate (top right) shows one satisfactory solution using wall-mounted lights. In some cases, however, high-mast lighting is the only possible way in which adequate lighting levels can be obtained, as at this traffic interchange in Newport, Monmouthshire.

Appropriate modern light fittings can generally be found for most sites and can range from the exuberant multiple type, such as this Swedish example (above left) to the simpler and more self-effacing variety, like the Norwich pattern shown here (above right).

Lighting such as this in Guildford, Surrey (below left) can be used for general illumination both in built-up areas and elsewhere. The other examples (below centre and right) are from Amsterdam and Boston, Massachusetts, respectively and are clearly intended as decorative features – the Amsterdam example by day as much as by night.

While modern light fittings are appropriate in most, if not all, sites (above left) it would be a pity to lose existing and characterful lights like these (above right) in the centre of Brussels, which have actually been updated using modern halogen sources, or those shown below in Cardiff (left) and Elm Hill in Norwich.

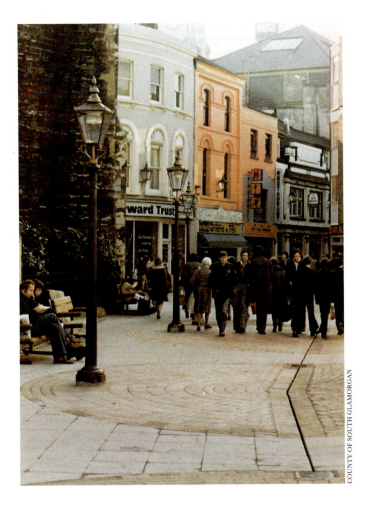

Vandalism and public lighting systems

by Ken Shaw TENG(CEI), DMS, AMBIM, Senior Assistant Engineer (Lighting), London Borough of Greenwich.

There is a growing awareness that acts of vandalism are costing Britain millions of pounds each year, either in repairing the initial damage or in finding ways and means by which the worst effects of it can be minimised.

Significantly, two of the most important features of vandalism are that it appears to affect mainly public rather than private property, and that many of the more serious offences – arson for example – take place at night. Not surprisingly, at a time when local authorities are grappling with increased demands for services and the additional drain on resources that this implies, there is an increasing concern about the scale of the problem and about finding ways of reducing it.

What is vandalism?

When a Government report defined vandalism as 'wilful and malicious damage to public and private property without clear advantage to the perpetrator', it was expressing an almost universal view. Yet this report, and many others, produces a strange hotchpotch of offences ranging from damage caused during a burglary to that inflicted by children at play. Clearly these need to be categorised in some way, otherwise the search for predisposing causes will ultimately fail.

Criminal damage offences can be divided into five main types: play, acquisitive, malicious, vindictive and tactical. The level of protection that is necessary with respect to the first two types is a matter of assessment against the immediate costs involved in taking steps to protect the property and/or equipment. It is the remaining acts, however, on which the majority of costs hinge, for vast sums of money are spent on repairing acts of criminal damage to industrial, commercial and public premises, much of which takes place at night. In one area alone – that of industrial and commercial premises – in 1976 there were more than 250,000 break-ins, the cost of which, including vandalism, was put at £400 million. Arson, for example, is the most common cause of fires in schools, and yet artificial lighting here is rarely considered.

Most commentators today accept that vandalism has a combination of causes and many factors are thought to be contributory. Environmental factors such as school, work and leisure surroundings are quoted on the one hand, while emotional needs such as levels of boredom, personal relationships and frustration are quoted on the other. Some people believe that social and physical deprivation are most significant, while others suggest that the built environment and the effect of building size, shape, type and degree of community control are even more so.

Who are the vandals?

The vandal is nearly always seen as a male adolescent, and a whole range of behaviour is attributed to this one type; however, no single category predominates. For example, nearly two thirds of telephone vandals are adults whose main objective is theft; much railway vandalism (such as putting objects on the lines) is carried out by children between the ages of 8 and 12.

In 1972 the Home Office Research Unit set up four studies to tackle vandalism. One carried out in Blackburn found that children up to the age of 12 or so accounted for 33 per cent of the reported vandalism. Play vandalism tended to take the form of throwing stones, climbing trees, scribbling, and so on. It is worth adding that the main offenders acted in small groups and did not go on to commit other crimes. The peak age of male offenders brought to the notice of the police (not just those brought to Court) was less than 10.

A second project in Liverpool found that 48 per cent of the 600 children interviewed claimed to have broken a street lamp in the previous six months, and many of them more than one. If half the boys in Liverpool are breaking a street lamp every six months, the cost is obviously high.

Reducing vandalism

Lighting is important at the outset; it remains one of the most socially acceptable means of minimising vandalism there is today. Unfortunately when it is considered at the moment it is usually spoken of in its narrowest sense as an aid to detection. It is rarely thought of as an active means by which increased social activity could be used to police the space, or in its widest sense as one of the first rational steps towards good economic housekeeping in the utilisation of capital-intensive recreational projects.

Over the whole field of human activities, street and environmental lighting improves amenity. It generates greater pedestrian movement and the benefit of perhaps the greatest importance in environmental areas is that the increased surveillance opportunities that artificial lighting affords have a demonstrable effect in reducing irrational fears and anxieties.

Street lights are both an object of vandalism and a deterrent against it. In high-risk areas, the importance of street lighting to deter vandalism cannot be overstressed. Damage to the lighting fittings themselves can be reduced by a combination of careful choice and siting of equipment, and regular checking and maintenance.

Choice of suitable equipment

Protecting equipment by improved construction or by the use of more vandal-resistant materials are the most widespread approaches aimed at limiting vandalism. The two most vulnerable areas are the luminaire and the column door.

It is now nearly 30 years since acrylic plastics began to replace glass in the lighting industry. Unfortunately both materials shatter and neither can form an effective shield against vandalism. However with the introduction of UV stabilised polycarbonate and the development of injection moulding techniques, it is possible for manufacturers to produce luminaire bowls incorporating accurate optical systems and to fabricate sophisticated fastening arrangements into the bowl assemblies, thereby providing benefits in terms of reduced costs, strength and ease of maintenance.

Following the introduction of electric lighting, there has been a major change in the use of materials in column design, brought about to a large extent by the development of higher mounting heights for traffic route lighting. This, together with the recent rapid increase in illuminated street furniture, has meant that much of the control equipment and supply terminations have had to be housed in a compartment at low level.

However, little attention has been given to the problems associated with the accessibility of column compartments and their vulnerability to attack. In this respect modern doors are far from satisfactory; almost without exception they can be simply levered off, leaving expensive equipment exposed to the weather and further attack.

Bearing in mind the high cost of damage caused through the removal of doors from street furniture, it is clearly time to reconsider our current attitudes to column design. Many installations lend themselves to the adoption of different techniques in combating vandalism, and we could certainly design more of our installations using methods which avoid the use of column doors. For instance:

1 Flush-mounted pavement boxes or service points within a secure building or other enclosure could be used to control wall-mounted luminaires or doorless columns.

2 Groups of adjacent lighting/sign points could be controlled

CONCRETE UTILITIES LTD

KEN SHAW

Light fittings are not only a target for vandals (above right) but, once broken, other acts of vandalism are facilitated after dark. Low-level lighting can alternatively be provided by illuminated bollards (above left) which can be made virtually vandal proof by careful design and construction. High-level lighting used in London's Leicester Square has its control gear built into the lanterns themselves, and so is less vulnerable to damage, but it needs proper equipment for servicing and replacement.

DESIGN COUNCIL

from service chambers similar in design to Post Office inspection pits.

3 Illuminated signs could be mounted on straight posts or on lighting columns, from which they could then be controlled.

4 With the introduction of concentric cables and luminaires with integral gear, smaller cut-outs mounted on the shaft of the column could be used, accessible only by means of a compact door, out of reach of children with busy hands.

Certain other aspects should be borne in mind when choosing suitable lighting fittings:

1 Equipment should be purchased only if it complies with the relevant British Standard.

2 Catches, toggles, bolts and locks used to fasten the equipment in position need to be sturdy and made from non-corrosive materials.

3 Protective coatings should be able to withstand normal wear and tear and have a certain degree of resistance to attack, the main forms being graffiti, scratching and peeling.

4 Bare bulbs must obviously be protected by a suitable lantern bowl.

Siting of equipment

The second area for consideration is the lighting layout – in other words designing features into the layout which counter vandalism in its early stages. When lighting columns and electrical equipment are placed alongside walls or low buildings, they provide climbing opportunities for children at play and enable other equipment to be reached for further vandalism or possibly other criminal acts. When equipment is out of sight, behind lock-up garages, for example, there is a greater chance of its being tampered with and damaged. Where possible positions such as these should be avoided.

It is sometimes possible to counter vandalism by putting the light source out of reach. The main advantages of using high-level lighting are that it maintains the daylight appearance of the environment; that it reduces the number of targets for attack; and that it can provide a high level of general lighting. The main disadvantages are that in practice the result tends to be cold and unsympathetic; that supplementary lighting is nearly always required; that fixing luminaries to building structures will not normally provide adequate levels of light on steps or in alleyways; and that problems of glare may be difficult to overcome.

Where possible equipment should not be installed until the site is ready. The column or guard post must be planted firmly in position. In the case of a lighting installation, the lantern(s) should be left off until the service can be connected. Lighting equipment installed on an occupied, lit site is less likely to be vandalised. Rubbish should be removed, as it may provide ammunition.

Maintenance

The relationship between maintenance and vandalism is important. The formal diagnosis of what is or is not vandalism depends on the maintenance engineer. Good feed-back on the deterioration of equipment is essential, since minor faults and repairs can develop and encourage wilful damage. Indeed, what sometimes passes for urban vandalism is simply inadequate maintenance.

So information concerning the environment is important for a number of reasons: initially because it provides the basic data for organisations such as local authorities to operate (quantities, descriptions, locations, age of materials, plant and equipment etc); but later on because it provides a yardstick by which performance or standards can be measured.

The levels and degree of vandalism and its cost to the community, therefore, form just one important aspect of the overall picture. Yet, surprisingly enough, no one has yet tried to use this data to assess how damage is accelerated by inadequate maintenance or through the degeneration of obsolete equipment, nor have they considered the effect that the increase in the sheer number of targets over the past few years has had on it.

There can be few industries whose equipment and plant are continually subject to inclement weather, corrosion, accidental and wilful damage and sheer hard wear who give so little attention to preventive maintenance. But with the greater involvement today of supervisory staff in administration, brought about by the growing complexity of lighting systems generally and incentive schemes in particular, more attention will need to be paid in the future to maintenance management. Certainly a planned maintenance cycle involving a full electrical, mechanical and structural inspection is needed to assess the effect and extent of wilful and accidental damage as well as the natural deterioration of equipment.

It is widely accepted that good illumination is probably one of the most important tools in preventing crime, but its effect in reducing vandalism to other sections of the community is rarely considered. Yet if high levels of illumination were provided in high-risk areas, vandals would be more likely to be seen and thus discouraged from antisocial activities. At present security lighting is primarily thought of as being a deterrent to industrial or commercial crime. The scope for using amenity lighting techniques objectively as a deterrent to social crimes is still virtually untapped.

One area where amenity lighting might be used more is to enable the night use of play and recreational facilities, where this can be done without the generation of adverse side effects such as noise and disturbance. Many capital-intensive community projects could in this way be put to more economic use as well as channelling youthful and adult energies into socially acceptable activities.

Perhaps when engineers, architects and planners alike get around to thinking of the outdoor environment as a place for people and not just cars; for children and not just for adults; for play and recreational activities and not just for sport; we might find that in passing we have also gone some way in helping to find a solution to vandalism.

Perhaps the most vandal-resistant solution to lighting layouts is to fix general light sources to nearby buildings, as at this street junction in Norwich (left), but supplementary lighting may still be needed and there may be glare and supply problems. Low-level fittings are always open to attack (below left) and even modern materials and designs may not be satisfactory. The doors on lamp columns are often a particularly weak point (below right). Designs could be improved in many cases, but poor maintenance, leaving covers off or attaching them temporarily is an open invitation to further damage and will seldom protect the equipment inside (below centre).

KEN SHAW

KEN SHAW

DESIGN COUNCIL

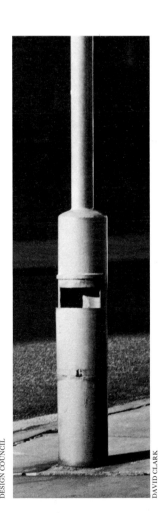

DAVID CLARK

47

Street furniture: what happens in practice

survey by Chris Swann and Francis Bridgeman,
Bath University.

Selecting and siting street furniture can never be a once-and-for-all affair. The simplest schemes evolve and expand with time, and the products used in them wear or break and have to be replaced, so there is a permanent problem of maintenance.

It was with this in mind that, in 1977, following a suggestion made by Professor Roy Worskett, City Architect and Planning officer for Bath, the Design Council arranged for two final-year architectural students from Bath University to carry out a general survey of selected urban sites in Bath itself, Frome, Exeter and Brighton. Their brief, which was worked out with the help of Professor Worskett and Professor Gregory of the School of Architecture, was to make an appraisal of all the street furniture, including paving surfaces and planting, under three main headings:

1 How well it survived in everyday use, including an assessment of such factors as appearance, siting, maintenance problems and resistance to damage and vandalism.
2 How well it was integrated visually, including comments on the original selection and siting decisions and on subsequent maintenance and replacement.
3 The general effect it had on the street scene and on people using it.

In addition, the students were asked to find out about the way in which responsibilities for selecting, installing and maintaining street furniture were structured, and how this related to what actually happened on site.

The survey programme began with two pilot visits: to the Southgate shopping centre, Bath; and to two areas in Frome, a residential development and Frome town centre. The students then carried out two full-scale surveys of sites in Exeter (Newtown GIA and the semi-pedestrianised High Street) and in Brighton (Hanover GIA and the Churchill Square shopping precinct). A final report, including a large number of photographs, was produced in Autumn 1977.

Clearly, it would be invidious to generalise from such a small sample, particularly with respect to general planning and maintenance policies. It is perhaps worth mentioning, however, that those concerned generally felt that more remote planning at county level took longer and cost more than a local system. The longer chain of command was felt to be wasteful and responsibilities were less clear cut.

To show the sort of information generated by the survey, here is one example of a product report from the Brighton area.

Site	—
Product	Bench
Number on site	100 approximately
Manufacturer	—
Materials and finishes	Natural hardwood slats fixed by flush-headed mild steel bolts to plastics-coated mild steel channel frames bolted to concrete below paving
Condition	All intact and serviceable, but not pristine
Damage and wear	Rusty bolt heads. Green growth on seats in shady positions. Plastics coating chipped on all seats and peeling off some, allowing frame to rust. Some frame welds failed and rewelded, causing rusting. Bolt heads protruding from bases in some cases
Integration	Modern lines fit in well, though a brighter colour might have enlivened the surrounding, mainly concrete, site. Bases fit flush in paving, but not always tidily. Seating areas effectively defined by change to brick paving
Performance	Very popular with public. Almost everybody found them comfortable for hard seats. Good choice of sunny, shady, busy or quiet sites

A number of general points emerge and are worth restating, bearing in mind that different sites and budgets will determine the initial choice of furniture. Taking each item of furniture in turn, here are some of the most frequent comments.

Surfaces
The greater the traffic, the harder surfaces needed to be to stand up well. Concrete blocks should be through-coloured (and checked to be so before laying). Poorly laid tarmac was a liability, and rolled gravel washed away easily in bad weather. Cobbles, contrary to expectations, did not hold litter, but were not liked by pedestrians (although, equally, people didn't always stop at 'barrier' strips of cobbles). Darker surfaces were favoured round seats and, possibly, large litter containers because they resisted staining. Soft surfaces should be provided in play areas, especially under high equipment. Yellow lines for parking restrictions were sometimes felt to be a problem

Tree grilles can often present problems. Not only do young trees seldom grow exactly as and where intended, but grilles frequently trap litter and loose gravel.

No matter whether surfaces are simple or decorative, they need to be maintained. London's Carnaby Street (above left) now looks decidedly tatty and is difficult to repair, but badly maintained details can be found in many less ambitious schemes as well (above right).

No waiting for motorists (below left) – and no room for pedestrians either! It would be easy enough to improve on siting like this. Initially sloppy installation (below centre) almost invariably makes subsequent maintenance more difficult. Damaged walls in the Southgate shopping centre in Bath (below right) were found to be caused by supermarket trolleys.

Seating appeared to be particularly vulnerable on most sites and was frequently difficult to remove for renovation when paint or galvanising began to deteriorate. Darker surfaces under seats helped to disguise stains.

and were often very intrusive visually; some authorities found tape lines effective, others preferred paint. Patent paving blocks needed careful laying, and too thick a layer of sand beneath them had given rise to problems in one case. Maintenance clearly needed more supervision in several cases: levels had been upset and new grouting round relaid areas seldom matched the original.

Seating

Seats and benches seemed to be the most vulnerable items of furniture (with the possible exception of litter bins). Plastics caps were missing from hollow section steel frames, causing them to corrode. Varnished wood slats lasted less well than, for instance, oiled teak. Plastics coatings also seemed vulnerable. In general it was felt that fixing seats flush with paving was aesthetically desirable, but bolted fixings allowed seats to be removed for renovation. It was generally appreciated when there was a choice of sunny and shady positions, and when there was something to look at – even other shoppers. Planting nearby and litter bins fairly close at hand (but not right next to the seats) were also liked.

Lighting

The proliferation of posts for lights and signs was often a problem. Mid-grey seemed to be a good colour for masking graffiti on posts. In general, and where this could be achieved, wall-mounted lights at high level were very unobtrusive by day and did a satisfactory job by night. Concrete columns showed spalling in some cases, and access panels in them were vandal prone. In Brighton, steel columns were found to have a short life in the salty atmosphere, and aluminium-coated steel required repainting every two or three years. Anodised aluminium, on the other hand, lasted for a dozen years and more without deterioration. Hinged bases were useful for maintenance where there was no access for trucks.

Bollards

Steel bollards and posts with plastics coatings rapidly began to look rather tatty, and concrete bollards with a definite texture seemed to last much better. Bollards were used successfully to denote routes for occasional vehicles through semi-pedestrianised areas. One detail point was that bollards should be set in surrounding surfaces to the correct design level, which meant picking the right size of bollard in the first place.

Litter bins

Litter always presents difficulties, even when it's put in bins. Concrete litter bins showed staining round weepholes in their bases, and there were often gaps between internal wire baskets and their surrounds. Plastic bags could be used to keep the inside of bins clean, but they were often improperly fitted round the top of bins and consequently looked untidy. Flimsy bins rarely lasted for any length of time, but wall-mounted bins were felt to be less vulnerable than free-standing or post-mounted ones. Fixing straps seemed to rust very easily. Lids were rarely effective in keeping insects away from bin contents. Larger bins seemed to be used more and yellow ones were easily visible – perhaps too easily in some areas. There seemed little point in providing bins in residential sites.

Signing

Once again, posts were a problem. Many signs were the responsibility of engineering departments; others belonged to highways, who generally preferred internal illumination, in spite of occasional problems with maintenance and water resistance. Wall mounting was felt to be preferable, especially for small 'no waiting' signs, with shared posts as second best.

Litter bins invariably take a pounding in busy areas, even in normal use. Vandalism can also be a problem, particularly where it is encouraged by poor cleaning and maintenance. Lids seemed to be of doubtful benefit and plastics liners, while simplifying emptying and reducing staining, rarely fitted bins which were not designed for them.

Planters can trap litter and make cleaning difficult, especially if they have undercut bottom edges and are placed in groups. Brick planters, on the other hand, can be made easy to clean and are relatively hard to damage, but do restrict subsequent rearrangement.

An extra coat of paint was apparently useful in helping to protect galvanising on steel railings and other items of street furniture. Handrails, however, were frequently positioned in such a way as to make repainting difficult.

On the other hand, posts had to be strong enough for the job where big signs were essential.

Planters and planting

Apart from holding plants and shrubs, planters inevitably became impromptu seats and litter bins. Worse, many models accumulated litter round their bases and were difficult to clean. Exeter made use of purpose-built brick planters (which had built-in watering points at low level) with some proprietary models in positions where they might have to be moved for traffic route changes. Sharp corners were both dangerous and easily chipped and damaged.

The planting itself clearly needed a lot of attention, particularly in the early stages. Once well established, vandalism and other damage seemed less likely. Some trees seemed to be more vulnerable than others: sycamore and maple and lime appeared relatively tough. Transplanting trees that were too large and doing it too late in the spring were common causes of failure.

Railings and fences

Galvanising was surprisingly often damaged, causing rusting of steel railings. An extra coat of paint seemed to help. Square sections discouraged children from using railings as impromptu swings and climbing frames. Railings and handrails should be positioned so that they can be repainted easily. Brighton has a policy of salvaging old railings from outlying areas and using them as replacements and for repairs in the middle of the town.

Posters and advertising

Poster units were generally in very good condition and well maintained. Bus shelters incorporating advertising also seemed to work well, though there had been maintenance problems in one area. Careful planning was clearly needed to ensure that all the relevant notices and signs on shelters were included from the start. People's opinions varied on the attractiveness and effectiveness of posters in shopping precincts, but they did add colour in some areas.

Other decorative elements

Architecture and shop fronts were not included in the survey, except in so far as they formed the background against which furniture was used. Two areas, however, included municipal artistic features. The success of these was difficult to judge; most people were puzzled rather than inspired or impressed. Perhaps something with a more local flavour would have been more successful.

Overall, first impressions of schemes are often strongest, and maintenance and cohesiveness play a very strong part in these. Bitty, unco-ordinated and grubby areas were partly the result of unclear planning and poor choice of product. Just as often, they seemed to be a reflection of a half-hearted attempt at improvement that had not been followed through and looked after enough – perhaps because the need for maintenance had been underestimated from the start.

One-off items of street furniture (top left) need particularly careful planning and installation – certainly more than in this case. Anodised aluminium lamp columns (top centre) were found to have the longest life in Brighton's sea air. Litter was a continual problem in Churchill Square shopping centre in Brighton (bottom left and centre) and was not helped by the fact that many corners were difficult to clean. Broken equipment (right) was frequently left in place for long periods, a danger to all and an encouragement to further damage.

Signing: confusion or clarity?

by Bob Kindred, Senior Planning Officer, Ipswich Borough Council.

It was Norbert Weiner who once said that the world may be viewed as an immense member of 'To Whom It May Concern' messages. This only becomes significant when we realise that every event and object in the environment, both past and present, has an identifying image which fills the world with messages. Signs that supply information are therefore a very important part of our surroundings, particularly when that information is supplied in a systematic way.

In recent years we have developed better methods of interpreting our environment, but there is much still to improve in the design and siting of the signing. In an increasingly complex world in which easy and speedy digestion of information is at a premium, signing must communicate clearly. The more at home a man is in his environment the less need he has for consciously designed sources of information. We now find ourselves strangers in our own cities, unable to see or understand how they work. It is the designer's job to clarify and regulate the flow of information so that priority signs cannot be missed and so that more accurate information is transmitted more easily and expressively.

In order to be effective as well as unobtrusive, signs must respect the environment in which they are situated, but on the other hand they must be separate from it to communicate. Visual order in signing systems is usually straightforward if shape and colour are applied with discrimination. In Reston, Virginia, roadside signage in parkland settings is attractive without being incongruous. It uses a substantial and infinitely variable arrangement of modular blocks in distinctive but muted colours. Messages can be either symbolically represented or written, although symbolic signs which are useful for speedy recognition or compactness are less successful when dealing with complex or abstract information. Symbol signs

are also unsatisfactory unless incorporated into an intelligent total system. The use of symbols alone, without consideration for the verbal messages and all other signage, only creates confusion. Once the basic systems have been clarified, sizes and locations of signs will be determined by principles of legibility, viewing angles and the logical sequence for observers in motion.

At the Hartford, Connecticut, Civic Centre the shopping, recreational and administrative facilities of the building have been provided on three floors, each of which is identified by signs of a particular colour. The logo for the centre is based on three semicircular bands of yellow, orange and brown, to represent the floors, and the top and bottom edges of each sign indicate how access is gained and on which level. The designers have also used Cooper Black for the lettering – a refreshing change from the merciless onslaught of Helvetica.

Systematic signage could be an outward expression of our public services in Britain but the overall standard of existing graphic design is poor. In some areas it is often discreet to the point of invisibility, with signing haphazardly designed and with information inconsistently and unimaginatively presented. Having failed to give a lead in environmental graphic design following reorganisation, local government seems scarcely to be in a position to give a lead in public signing, nor to define its requirements in the way of supplying information to the public. Few councils have been able to resist the introduction of an identifying logo or symbol, but the visual poverty of the results is clear evidence that few authorities have grasped the precepts of visual identity and how it could benefit them and their citizens. The failure to develop any worthwhile results from such exercises has perhaps made them less enthusiastic about producing signing systems for public facilities.

PAUL J. MYATT, WASHINGTON METROPOLITAN AREA TRANSIT AUTHORITY

DESIGN COUNCIL

IRVINE DEVELOPMENT CORPORATION

DESIGN COUNCIL

DESIGN COUNCIL

CHRIS SWANN/FRANCIS BRIDGEMAN

Signing systems clearly have to move beyond the perfunctory minimum – the functional pointing toward implied activities in obscure or unidentified buildings. In fact, overzealous signing programmes are already appearing here and there, but with the best intentions in the world have generally caused more confusion than clarity. Better signing can benefit an area in many ways: it can create awareness of facilities and opportunities; aid orientation and increase security in unfamiliar surroundings; tell of an area's history, ecology, and possible future development; and make the city more attractive and its parts more easy to identify.

Cities are large and complicated and people are increasingly mobile, so common knowledge is not sufficient. Orientation is easier when streets or areas have a distinct identity, and signing should reinforce the uniqueness of places and reflect the flow and activity of people. In central areas where people are clustered together, information signs can do the same; in parks and suburban neighbourhoods signing can be distinct, but dispersed and more subdued.

Information for people on foot should be designed to sustain both the casual glance and a prolonged study. It should be provided at important junctions; near transportation facilities, such as bus and rail stations and car parks; at focal points; and where there are high concentrations of people on foot. Presentation techniques should be simple and direct, combining words and pictures whenever possible, and should aim to show detailed descriptions and locations of nearby activities plus information on more general orientation and transport facilities. Supplementary information can vary in accordance with the particular interests of the audience.

Preparation and presentation of this kind of signage has been developed successfully in Washington DC and Boston. The Washington signage was developed for the Metro rapid transit system by Wyman and Cannan. It provides at each station twin illuminated maps showing both the entire transit system as it will be when completed, and a neighbourhood metro map based on a three-mile square around the station. The overall route map is highly stylised, making it difficult for people to orientate themselves with respect to important natural features such as parks and the Potomac River. The neighbourhood maps can offer greater information because of their larger scale, but despite this clarity there remains the conflict of presentation between the underground and the fine detail of the 'overground', which requires abstraction and oversimplification. In suburban areas facilities and services would not be so tightly clustered, so presentation problems would be less serious.

The map shows important landmarks, parks, tourist attractions, public and government buildings and facilities, with walking times from the station entrance. The artwork is silk-screened onto translucent styrene in such a way that it can accommodate the growth in the transit system and also show other changes in the area. As the system extends into suburban Virginia and Maryland, the maps are intended to reflect local facilities for each neighbourhood. It is likely that the designers, together with local planners and the Mass Transit Authority, should consult local community, special interest and minority groups to determine what information the maps will show before they are designed. A major disadvantage with the present system of signs is that they have only been installed at stations, rather than throughout the city centre, and they can only be consulted when the stations are open.

The Boston signage system consists of three-sided panels located at strategic points of maximum pedestrian movement and at transport facilities of all kinds throughout the city centre. Panels indicate the routes of the underground rapid transit system, the overall geography of Boston, and an enlarged extract of the area in which the sign is located. The extract is part map, part diagram and comprises a walking guide to the area, with indications of sites, landmarks, exhibits and information centres, rapid transit routes and walking trails. The displays are large enough in scale for the information to be useful and large enough in size to be legible. They are also simple enough, for all the information they seem to contain, for their content once extracted by the user to be retained and related to the immediate environment. The representation of the surroundings and the surroundings themselves are therefore experienced simultaneously. This has tremendous benefits, not only with the general information signs, but also with the historical information monoliths which show how the city has developed over time.

Where a lack of co-ordination between different kinds of signing system has occurred there have been efforts in the past to develop integrated hardware, as if this would lead to an equivalent integration of information. Where innovation is required, as in information systems for people on foot, components can either be adapted from standard ones or are too specialised to be manufactured for national consumption. The introduction of materials such as Metalphoto from America, where the reproduction of photographic material on aluminium sheet is common practice, may be one way in which innovative design work for signing can be done cheaply and effectively, but the needs of people in urban environments must be carefully determined before indiscriminate and insensitive signage systems are applied.

Opposite page: The Metro rapid transit system in Washington DC uses twin maps in stations to show both the entire transit system and (shown here, 1) a neighbourhood map of a 3-mile square around the station. A coded map (3) indicates the facilities in the 150 acre Beach Park at Irvine New Town in Scotland. The Eldon Square shopping precinct in Newcastle-upon-Tyne uses both symbols and words (2, 4 and 5) and contrasts with the confusion of signs (4) in Churchill Square, Brighton.

Pictograms and words are used in the signs in Glenrothes, Scotland (7). This sign (8) in the Waterfront Park in Boston, Massachusetts, gives the history of the area.

Haddenham won the Best Kept Village competition in East Cambridgeshire despite this array of signs and posts (9). Negative information on this bus stop in Doncaster (10) seems unhelpful. This row of signs in Newbury (11) could easily be co-ordinated to be tidier and simpler to absorb. Rustic design such as this on the Marlow by-pass (12) is out-of-place in such an environment, just as these three posts (13) seem excessive in London's Oxford Street. The obliteration of one sign by another is all-too-common: this example (14) is in Colchester.

ALL PICTURES DESIGN COUNCIL

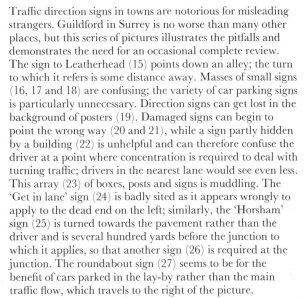

Traffic direction signs in towns are notorious for misleading strangers. Guildford in Surrey is no worse than many other places, but this series of pictures illustrates the pitfalls and demonstrates the need for an occasional complete review. The sign to Leatherhead (15) points down an alley; the turn to which it refers is some distance away. Masses of small signs (16, 17 and 18) are confusing; the variety of car parking signs is particularly unnecessary. Direction signs can get lost in the background of posters (19). Damaged signs can begin to point the wrong way (20 and 21), while a sign partly hidden by a building (22) is unhelpful and can therefore confuse the driver at a point where concentration is required to deal with turning traffic; drivers in the nearest lane would see even less. This array (23) of boxes, posts and signs is muddling. The 'Get in lane' sign (24) is badly sited as it appears wrongly to apply to the dead end on the left; similarly, the 'Horsham' sign (25) is turned towards the pavement rather than the driver and is several hundred yards before the junction to which it applies, so that another sign (26) is required at the junction. The roundabout sign (27) seems to be for the benefit of cars parked in the lay-by rather than the main traffic flow, which travels to the right of the picture.

57

The criteria for good traffic direction signs are that they should be easy to read, sturdy, economic to manufacture and maintain, and neat in appearance. But too often they end up looking like the signs shown above (28 and 29). Warrington New Town has tackled the problem with its own signing system (30) based on a rectangular plank mounted between two posts of rectangular section; the lighting gear is housed in another rectangular section and mounted above the signs to give some protection from the weather and

vandals. Traffic regulation signs and chevron boards are mounted on the face of the post (32), helping to produce a much tidier solution to the usual roundabout signing (31). The system works well for all kinds of signs (33 and 34, opposite page). Great care has been taken to ensure economy and ease of installation and maintenance, and experience has shown that this system is no more expensive than the system it has replaced.

Picture sequence

33 34 35

37   36

38   39

WARRINGTON NEW TOWN DEVELOPMENT CORPORATION

WARRINGTON NEW TOWN DEVELOPMENT CORPORATION

WARRINGTON NEW TOWN DEVELOPMENT CORPORATION

Warrington has also developed its own range of signs, this time for road names. These are in aluminium, with screen-printed graphics and stove enamelled. The posts are slotted to take inch-thick boards and can carry just the name (37) or can also have additional 'Leading to' board (35), which is held by bolts through the top board. The boards and posts are held together by a socket head bolt secured to a nut welded inside the post. Northampton Development Corporation (36, 38 and 39) has a similar system.

NORTHAMPTON DEVELOPMENT CORPORATION

WARRINGTON NEW TOWN DEVELOPMENT CORPORATION

NORTHAMPTON DEVELOPMENT CORPORATION

NORTHAMPTON DEVELOPMENT CORPORATION

59

DESIGN COUNCIL

DESIGN COUNCIL

MICHAEL MIDDLETON

DAVID CLARK

DESIGN COUNCIL

DESIGN COUNCIL

Some signs are meaningless, or, worse, totally confusing. What is an 'Environmental Area' and what is wrong with a conventional 'No through road' sign (40, Camden in London)? These parking restrictions (41, Southwold in Suffolk) provide an interesting puzzle for motorists wanting to stop, while American drivers are not even allowed to stop to decipher these signs in Michigan (42). These internally-lit signs in Paris are attractive, but may be a little too discreet for drivers (43). Contra-flow bus lanes have spawned their own signs too: this one in Durham (44) means that any traffic can travel in one direction but buses only in the other; but what does this sign (45, Kensington in London) mean, especially the time limitation? Drivers in Leeds (46) are confronted by a jungle of ill-mounted signs, while those in Islington in London (47) meet an entirely new sign to decipher. Pedestrians have problems too (48, Oxford Street in London).

DESIGN COUNCIL

DESIGN COUNCIL

DESIGN COUNCIL

Your street: for you or your car?

by Paul Burall, Design Council

The sidewalk or pavement has become a regular feature of the street scene only in the past hundred years or so, since the twin requirements of safety and cleanliness made it essential to separate pedestrians from other kinds of traffic. Previously, streets in towns and villages had been shared. Horses, carriages and carts moved as best they could among people on foot who used the street, not just to get from one place to another, but also as somewhere to talk, to buy and sell, and, in the case of children, to play.

Now the pavement is ubiquitous, an accepted part of the scene in city centre, town terrace, suburban estate and village street. Segregation is total: roads are for vehicles and pavements are for people. So rigid is the division that the danger which most parents fear more than any other is that of their child venturing onto the road outside their home. For roads are designed so that people and goods can travel from place to place at a minimum speed of 30 mph, and they are no place for a pedestrian.

The harmful effect of this hierarchy is at its most pronounced in residential areas, where fast-moving traffic inhibits such natural activities as mothers walking with prams, children playing, and neighbours visiting or just talking to each other in the street. Traffic engineers and planners have been trying various methods to alleviate the results of the vehicle/pedestrian conflict for many years now, with the Radburn system of segregating pedestrians and traffic being perhaps the most widely used.

Millers Court at Hammersmith in London is a small infill development of houses, with the road as a fully integrated part of the overall design. The change in surface colour and texture and the positioning of the planters clearly indicates to drivers that this is no ordinary thoroughfare and that they must drive with extra care.

Developed in the United States in the late 1920s, but most widely used in post-war Britain, the Radburn system entails having entirely separate systems of roads and footpaths in housing estates, with each home usually served by a footpath to the front door with vehicle access from a road at the rear. The theory is fine: pedestrians can walk freely, away from traffic, on paths where children can play safely, while vehicles can drive right up to each house on roads from which pedestrians are meant to be excluded. But many Radburn schemes fail to achieve their ideal. First, access for visitors arriving by car is too often through the kitchen, which is not popular. Second, and perhaps more fundamental, residents just will not leave the access roads for vehicles only: cars are washed and repaired; mothers take short cuts; children use the space for biking, football and skateboarding. People just will not behave in certain ways just to please planners, particularly near their own homes in areas where they feel that the space is theirs, to use as they see fit.

So what are the roads around houses really for? Is it essential for people to be able to drive up to their front doors at 30 mph? Or should the whole area around a house – including the road – be considered as living space, an extension of the home? After all, substantial parts of most housing estates are made up of roads, often more than 25 per cent of the whole, which is a considerably larger proportion than is usually given over to public open space. That alone is reason enough for questioning the devotion of road space solely to the convenience of the car.

One-way streets are renowned for encouraging fast driving. Rochdale has a sensible solution by using nose-in parking (above), the angled rear of the parked vehicles acting as a threat to speed and, incidentally, giving pedestrians crossing between parked cars a good view of oncoming vehicles.

Britain's first shared space scheme at The Brow in Runcorn (below) is designed to give drivers deliberately short sight-lines to ensure that they travel slowly.

Questions such as these have now prompted a new approach, typified in Britain by the pioneering work carried out in the Cheshire New Town of Runcorn.

Runcorn's first housing, completed in 1966, was traditional Radburn plan and suffered the usual disadvantages of being 'misused' by residents who neither knew nor cared about the Radburn theory of how they were meant to behave. Inspired by an imaginative engineer responsible for site development, Mr Eddie Jenkins, the Runcorn designers abandoned Radburn and segregation and decided to try a completely new approach for their next housing project, The Brow. The result was the first residential estate to be designed as a pedestrian area into which vehicles are allowed only on sufferance.

Within The Brow are 266 houses served by four culs-de-sac off a local distributor road. The distributor is an ordinary carriageway six metres wide with all the excellent sight-lines associated with a road designed for vehicles travelling at 30 mph, and as such marks the edge of the pedestrian area. The culs-de-sac are very different: here children play, mothers stroll with prams, elderly people whose eyesight or hearing may be failing walk or chat; cars, refuse lorries, and delivery vans creep along at no more than 10 to 15 mph, their drivers well aware that here they are trespassing in an area where they do not have priority.

Yet there are no signs limiting speed or warning of children playing in the road, nor are there any 'sleeping policemen' or other mechanical devices to slow vehicles. The success of The Brow has been achieved by designing the culs-de-sac in a way that creates an overall impression which indicates to drivers and pedestrians alike that this is no ordinary road but a part of the living space of an essentially residential area. The culs-de-sac vary in width from about three metres to around six metres; thick planting is taken right up to the edge of the road surface and this combines with slopes and curves to restrict sight-lines severely; there are no separate footpaths along the edge of the road, thus avoiding any indication of vehicle priority. Parking is in small courts off the culs-de-sac, with space for both visitors and residents to leave their cars close to the front of each house. A separate footpath system crosses the culs-de-sac at right angles and provides the link between houses, schools, shops and Runcorn's segregated busway system.

The philosophy of The Brow has been used in all subsequent residential developments in Runcorn, including the 2200-home Castlefields development, where some culs-de-sac are 300 metres long and serve up to 100 dwellings each. Even here, the designers have successfully created an environment within which drivers slow down naturally, perceiving that they are intruding into a living area, and are unworried about taking an extra half minute or so to drive the length of the cul-de-sac at 10 to 15 mph rather than the usual 30 mph. The other controlling factor is, of course, the amount of traffic using each cul-de-sac. In The Brow, a survey showed that the maximum traffic generated by the 206 dwellings was some 100 vehicles in the peak hour, or a maximum average of less than one vehicle every two minutes along any one cul-de-sac. Clearly even slow, narrow culs-de-sac can cope with traffic well above this level, and experience elsewhere in Britain has shown that a cul-de-sac can be shared satisfactorily by vehicles and pedestrians even when the number of vehicles per hour reaches 100 or even 150 in the peak.

The Runcorn philosophy of creating residential areas in which vehicles are clearly intruding into a living area and have no priority has been taken up and developed in other parts of Britain and, indeed, abroad. But one essential characteristic of the Runcorn culs-de-sac remains almost unique to the New

Town: this is the recognition that it is the overall form of the total residential environment which the driver, and the pedestrian, perceive and which then determines whether they treat the area as one primarily for pedestrians or for vehicles. Thus the Runcorn team resolutely refuse to quantify the geometry of what makes a satisfactory cul-de-sac: they believe that the architect, the engineer and the landscape architect can only create the right visual effect by working together as a team on each individual site. The effectiveness of the Runcorn philosophy depends as much on the visual relationship between buildings, landscaping and the contours of the site as on any magic radii or gradients for the road.

What is more, the Runcorn designers are prepared to amend their thinking to fit in with the way in which people actually behave on site. For example, refuse lorries were supposed not to use the culs-de-sac in The Brow but to collect from the distributor road. However, the crews soon found it easier to drive into the parking courtyards via the culs-de-sac, damaging some of the landscaped road edges in the process. Instead of trying to persuade the crews to revert to the planner's intention, the Runcorn team accepted the change and simply put down a few extra granite setts to protect the landscaped edges.

The Runcorn team has no design rules. They virtually devise a new solution for each site, their only guidelines being that each system must satisfy three basic tests: first it must be safe not just for the alert pedestrian but for the distracted mother, the day-dreaming child, and the partially-sighted old person; second it must work, providing access where people want it and not making them park 50 metres from their front door; and third it must be environmentally acceptable, feeling right for all who use it. Perhaps the biggest compliment to the

No driver can enter this small cul-de-sac in Warrington (above) without realising that he is leaving an ordinary road and entering a special area. Changes in surface are also used in this housing scheme (below) in the United States to indicate an area where pedestrians and vehicles mix. Planting, choice of surface, and the overall scale of the detailing help to emphasise that these are places where people live, where kids play in the roadway, where neighbours stand and chat, and where the car moves only on sufferance.

DESIGN COUNCIL

DESIGN COUNCIL

Careful attention to detail and to scale are essential if vehicles and pedestrians are to share the same space safely. Signs are unnecessary; indeed, their presence would be an admission of failure. Thus the white line in the centre of the cul-de-sac at Runcorn (above left) peters out after a few yards, having served its purpose of indicating the junction with the distributor road. Again, where the footpath network crosses a cul-de-sac at Runcorn (above right), a change in surface colour and narrowing of the road warns drivers to expect bikes and pedestrians crossing.

The Department of the Environment (below) shows how a cul-de-sac can be created in a road built for through traffic. Again, the surface change warns drivers that they are entering an essentially residential area, the message being reinforced by the tree planting, the bends in the road, and the narrowed carriageway.

DEPARTMENT OF THE ENVIRONMENT

Parked cars are involved in about a half of all pedestrian accidents in residential areas. The likelihood of children running out from between parked vehicles into the path of a lorry or car and being injured is obviously considerably less in an area where vehicles are encouraged to travel slowly. But ways of keeping parked cars off the roadway are nevertheless vital to the success of any scheme. Exeter (above left) and Warrington (above right) offer two solutions.

Access for emergency vehicles is often a problem when pedestrianising an area or closing a road to through traffic. The Department of the Environment suggests one attractive answer (below) in its bulletin *Residential roads and footpaths*.

65

work of the Runcorn designers is that the people who live in the culs-de-sac rarely comment on it or treat it as anything out of the ordinary.

Other planners have codified the shared culs-de-sac approach of Runcorn, perhaps recognising that the success of Runcorn's rule-less flexible approach might not work with a design team that possibly had not the time, the devotion, or the understanding of the New Town's planners. Two County Councils which have done much to promote the culs-de-sac philosophy both for local authority and private housing schemes are Cheshire and Essex.

Cheshire published its *Design Aid: Housing Roads* in 1976 and, while suggesting satisfactory geometrical standards for different kinds of roads in residential areas, stresses that 'Standards have a tendency to become rigid, limiting regulations. This is to be avoided. These Cheshire standards should be regarded as a flexible, creative tool.' The Essex *Design Guide for Residential Areas* was published in 1973 and it also emphasises that the intention is to establish a framework 'within which a more varied and imaginative approach to housing area design can be fostered'. Both guides recommend the use of contrasting surfaces for culs-de-sac and mews courts to differentiate areas shared by vehicles and pedestrians from conventional vehicle-priority roads. They also recommend the use of ramps to indicate to drivers that they are entering an area where they do not have priority.

Cheshire County Council has also tackled one of the most difficult objections to the shared culs-de-sac philosophy, the

The Essex *Design guide for residential roads* recommends the use of contrasting surfaces (below) to differentiate areas shared by vehicles and pedestrians from conventional vehicle-priority roads.

provision of services by the public utilities. The problem arises from the reluctance of the public utilities to provide services except under a footway or clear verge running alongside a road, which they claim ensures that access to services is comparatively easy. Cheshire has negotiated a joint agreement with all the public utilities serving the County which ensures the maximum cooperation in servicing areas where the demands of the utilities might conflict with the ideal overall environmental design.

The Cheshire scheme suggests shared trenches where possible; recognises that landscaping must be designed so that services are at a consistent depth and free from planting which might cause access or maintenance problems; accepts that in mews courts and certain other areas the services will have to be placed under the roadway; recognises that the geometry of access roads that also provide routes for services should take account of the necessary minimum radii for gas and water pipes and the need for sewers to follow straight lines between manhole covers; and places the responsibilities for providing adequate routes for services, complete with necessary agreements, with the developer. The Cheshire guide also emphasises the need for adequate marking of service routes and for advice to residents about the need to avoid any planting or building which could damage the services or prevent access for excavations.

Attempts to negotiate a national agreement on similar lines to that achieved in Cheshire have failed, largely because the utilities were unwilling to sign away their statutory rights to lay services in public highways and other public land without such comprehensive safeguards as to militate against the satisfactory design of residential areas based on the shared culs-de-sac or mews court principle. However, several authorities have found that working out solutions for individual sites with the local staff of the utilities can be entirely successful. Indeed, Essex County Council, having set about negotiating a Cheshire-style agreement, has now decided against this overall approach in favour of the advantages of flexibility of dealing with each site separately.

Developments in Runcorn, Cheshire and Essex have now been followed by a new Department of the Environment Bulletin *Residential roads and footpaths*. This takes a notably cautious view of 'innovative solutions, in particular those for the use of shared surfaces and narrow carriageways and for reducing vehicle speeds which have only been in use for a short time. It has been necessary therefore to balance the desire to encourage innovation with caution on some issues where matters of safety or the risk of increased expenditure on maintenance may be involved.' Nevertheless, the Bulletin also warns against the opposite extreme: 'It will normally be both unrealistic and uneconomic to plan for the worst imaginable driver and pedestrian behaviour and the worst possible combination of events'. The Bulletin also makes clear that official thinking now accepts the basic objectives of giving the needs of pedestrians priority over those of vehicles within residential areas.

The DoE Bulletin includes a valuable section on the waste of land which can result from an unimaginative and inflexible use of building lines, road geometry and so on, pointing out that this is not only uneconomic but tends to leave strips of land and over-large roadside corners which have no purpose and are difficult to maintain. It is this kind of thoughtlessly rigid application of the New Streets By-Laws and other rules which characterises too many post-war housing estates in Britain, with their featureless wide carriageways, over-generous junctions and patches of waste grass, all planned to allow a few cars to travel without hindrance at 30 mph.

Safety has always been the prime reason used by the road engineers to justify their rigid rules. But the DoE Bulletin points out that 90 per cent of accidents in large towns occur on primary district and local distributor roads, whereas access-only residential roads account for only 10 per cent. Nevertheless, a half of all accidents involving children aged less than five occur in residential roads. But the important point here is that most of those accidents are on the traditional 30 mph residential roads and that very few such accidents occur in culs-de-sac or other types of short link, even those serving up to 80 houses. The implication is obvious: a child who is not old enough to recognise the traditional priority of vehicles is at considerably greater risk in a road where the driver is encouraged by the designers to travel at 30 mph and to assume priority than in a cul-de-sac which is clearly a part of the residents' living space. The avoidance of long stretches of straight road by the use of culs-de-sac, short loops, T-junctions or even mini-roundabouts is suggested by the DoE to reduce vehicle speeds; changes in road surface and gradients, the use of closely spaced buildings and narrow gateways are also considered helpful. The Bulletin highlights the need to avoid parking on the carriageway, since up to half the pedestrian accidents in residential areas involve a parked vehicle.

One recently completed survey in Dalston, London, where traffic management measures were taken to exclude through traffic from a General Improvement Area showed a reduction of some 50 per cent in pedestrian accidents and about 25 per cent in vehicle-only accidents. More surprising, the number of accidents in the distributor and boundary roads around the GIA dropped significantly too.

The DoE Bulletin is particularly cautious about shared surfaces, claiming that the lack of empirical evidence, the very frequency of vehicles meeting pedestrians, and the fact that pedestrians have no legal precedence over vehicles are all reasons for restraint. Eight conditions for the design of shared surfaces are suggested:

1 the beginning of the shared surface should be clearly distinguished from the adjacent carriageway, for example by a change in texture or level

2 within the shared surface pedestrian and vehicular routes should not be differentiated

3 the shared surface should be in the form of a short cul-de-sac or loop carrying very low traffic volumes, and where the speeds adopted by drivers will be sufficiently low to enable them to give way to pedestrians

4 within the shared surface a clear zone free from parked cars should be provided of sufficient width to allow pedestrians and vehicles to pass comfortably

5 parking spaces should be clearly demarcated

6 a threshold should be provided between the shared surface and any adjacent entrances to dwellings or garages from which emerging drivers or pedestrians can see and be seen by approaching traffic. Intervisibility should also be provided between pedestrians and approaching vehicles at the junctions between shared surfaces and footways or footpaths

7 where dwellings are likely to contain children, gardens and/or nearby play areas should be provided to obviate the need for the shared surface to be used as a main location for play

8 the shared surface should be sufficiently well lit after dark to enable drivers to see potential obstacles such as changes in level, and for drivers and pedestrians to see each other

The problem of the adequate lighting of shared surfaces is considerable, for ideally the system should not only enable drivers to see pedestrians but should also be of a contrasting character to ordinary street lighting to help to distinguish the shared surface area from a traditional road. The lighting and the actual fittings should also be of a scale and design suitable for a residential area. Many planners believe that the fittings at present available are unsatisfactory for this purpose and are looking for new types.

It is obviously easier to design an entirely new housing area on the basis of creating a safe environment which is not dominated by vehicles than to convert an existing residential area. But the need is often even greater in existing residential streets, not least because the general lack of amenities in a deprived area can make the street a valuable space for landscaping and other amenities. The Department of the Environment, in its Area Improvement Note 9 *Traffic in General Improvement Areas*,

Traditional road layouts (bottom left) that are unimaginative and make inflexible use of building lines and road geometry not only waste valuable land but leave roadside strips and over-large roadside corners that have no purpose and are difficult to maintain. Such layouts are uneconomic and simply allow a few cars to travel at 30 mph or more in areas where such speeds are anyway

unwelcome and unnecessary. The Essex Design Guide mews court (bottom right) wastes no space: indeed, even the road surface itself can be used for play and other activities as well as for vehicular access. The Runcorn culs-de-sac have shown how as many as a 100 dwellings can be served satisfactorily by a winding, narrow road shared with pedestrians and with no adjacent footpaths.

The most comprehensive system for giving pedestrians priority over vehicles in residential streets has been developed in Holland, such areas being designated as Woonerfs. The entrance to each Woonerf is marked by a special sign (above left) and the road layout and street furniture is designed to emphasise the subservient role of vehicles. These signs indicating parking areas are discreetly set into the paving (above right) as bolder signs would begin to suggest a conventional street. Sufficient space for car parking is essential to the success of a Woonerf (below).

accepts this view and makes the prime point that progress can only begin if extraneous traffic is excluded and only vehicles with business in the residential area are allowed in. Even then, through traffic can be discouraged from individual streets, and on-street parking reduced. Various design measures to discourage traffic and create an environment that enhances the essential human scale of a residential area are recommended by the DoE and are beginning to be put into practice by local authorities in several parts of Britain.

But by far the most comprehensive and whole-hearted commitment to the philosophy of giving people priority over vehicles has come from Holland. There, helped by the fact that the traditional Dutch brick-paved street requires re-laying every five years or so, the appearance of residential streets has undergone a dramatic transformation, aided by a complete new set of traffic regulations introduced in 1976 to codify traffic priorities within what the Dutch now call a 'Woonerf' (defined as a residential area in which traffic is not allowed to dominate and where the special layout and street furniture emphasise the prime function of the area as being a place where people live).

The entrance to each Woonerf is indicated by a special sign. Within the Woonerf the usual traffic priorities are, by law, reversed. Pedestrians may use the full width of the highway and playing in the roadway is permitted. Drivers of all vehicles are restricted to walking speed and must take special heed of children at play. Neither drivers nor pedestrians are allowed to impede each other, and pedestrians must if necessary make way to allow a vehicle past. Finally, drivers can only park in areas marked for the purpose; within a Woonerf, an unmarked area means 'no parking'.

This legal recognition of the special nature of a residential road has obvious attractions. But both the Department of the Environment and many of the other British authorities with experience of shared surfaces feel that legislation is unnecessary, as the success of the philosophy depends on the design being self-enforcing: if legislation is needed to make drivers treat the area as intended, then the design has failed. The Dutch, in practice, accept this point and one of their publications, *Woonerf*, says: 'The design of a Woonerf must be such that it is absolutely apparent that the pedestrian, rather than the traffic, has the dominant role . . . the design should serve both to support and emphasise the traffic regulations.' Nevertheless, it is worth pointing out that the objectors to legal enforcement of pedestrian priority are also often reluctant to allow the imaginative use of street furniture to provide the visual indication required to make shared surfaces work properly. For example, a planting box at the entrance to a residential cul-de-sac will help self-enforcement, yet is frowned on by the legislators who insist that it is marked with 'keep left' signs and other traditional main road paraphernalia, thus negating the message that this is an area for pedestrians and not an ordinary road.

What is especially significant about the Dutch Woonerf system is the emphasis on the visual perception of the driver, ensuring that he automatically recognises the environment as one within which the vehicle is the intruder and the pedestrian has dominance. Thus it is stressed that anything, such as long kerbs or footpaths, which gives any indication of pedestrian/vehicle segregation must be avoided. Sleeping policemen, sharp bends and narrow sections of roadway are all recommended as means of slowing vehicles, while long sight-lines which encourage higher speeds are avoided. While play areas should be physically separated from areas where vehicles are allowed, they should not be so clearly defined as to create an impression that children cannot play elsewhere in the Woonerf. The overall visual effect of the Woonerf should be pleasant and appropriate to a residential area in which people can stroll, talk, sit and relax, and play. Trees and shrubs, varied paving materials, small-scale street furniture, occasional racks for bikes and mopeds are all recommended to help create the appropriate environmental feel.

The Dutch identify the prime difficulty of creating a Woonerf in an existing residential area as the need to find sufficient off-street parking. Where this is not possible, the Woonerf principle should be dropped, for 'cars will be parked regardless of parking regulations and thus destroy many of the concepts integral to the Woonerf'. The other major restraint on a Woonerf is that the maximum traffic load should not exceed 100–300 vehicles per hour, depending on the particular local characteristics. The Dutch also suggest that drivers are willing to travel at severely restricted speeds within a Woonerf for up to 500m, although recent studies have suggested that this figure may, in some circumstances, be optimistic.

The special Dutch laws that cover a Woonerf specify that, on those parts of the highway intended for use by vehicles, features must be introduced that will restrict the speed of all types of vehicle. Such features should be not more than 50 metres apart and can include twists, constrictions or humps in the roadway. Experience has shown that such features should be related to vertical elements in the overall design, and that any twists must be fairly severe to be effective. It is also important that the street is designed to ensure that vehicles do not pass close to buildings along the street, both for safety and environmental reasons; the Dutch suggest that 0.6 metres is the minimum gap.

ANWB

The whole purpose of a Woonerf is to make the street a pleasant place for pedestrians (above). but, of course, there still has to be adequate access for delivery and other large vehicles (below).

On costs, the Dutch suggest that the cost of a Woonerf-style new development is no greater than for a more conventional one, a fact borne out by schemes in Britain. But the Dutch experience that the creation of a Woonerf in an existing street will cost no more than 150 per cent of the cost of a major road repair scheme is unlikely to be valid elsewhere, simply because of the special way in which streets in Holland are built to allow for the very high water table.

With some eight years of experiment behind them, the Dutch summarise the advantages and disadvantages of the shared road surface philosophy as:

1 the Woonerf is inherently safer than other types of residential street

2 the environment of a Woonerf is more conducive to such activities as children's play and neighbourly contact

3 the system provides a safer environment for children to learn about traffic

4 in areas where land is restricted the Woonerf principle can provide much-needed space for landscaping and other public amenities

5 the cost, especially in older streets, is not cheap

6 the Woonerf design has little or no effect on the speed of mopeds and motorbikes, which remain a problem

The Dutch faith in the philosophy is emphasised by another final disadvantage they suggest: that the system is so attractive that residents who live in areas which are unsuitable for conversion into a Woonerf will feel frustrated that they cannot gain the benefits.

It is clear that the shared surface philosophy is now well past the pioneering stage and that its use in both new and existing residential areas is likely to spread rapidly. Indeed, probably the biggest risk to the success of the philosophy is that it will become a fashion and that the curves, slopes, shrubs, textured surfaces, bollards, seats and other ingredients which make up the successful schemes will be adopted with little regard for the underlying principles or for the particular needs of individual sites. Shared surface schemes only work if they take account of the way people actually behave; the imposition of artificial patterns of behaviour in the way that many Radburn layouts attempt will not only fail, but will be positively dangerous.

Perhaps the biggest challenge is to the traffic engineers. They are used to designing for vehicles whose performance is both well known and defined by regulations and whose drivers are constrained by accepted and enforcable rules. But pedestrians do not recognise rules; neither do they meet any construction and use regulations. So when dealing with the design of shared surfaces the traffic engineer has to produce solutions based more on the study of human behaviour than on prescribed physical or aesthetic criteria. Fortunately, experience in Runcorn and elsewhere has shown that engineers and planners can make this leap very successfully.

Design Aid: Housing Roads, price £1.00 from Cheshire County Council, Backford Hall, Nr Chester CHI 6EA

Design Guide for Residential Areas, price £4.50 from Essex County Council, County Hall, Chelmsford CM1 1LF

DoE Bulletin 32, *Residential roads and footpaths*, price £3.00 from HMSO

DoE Area Improvement Note 9, *Traffic in General Improvement Areas*, price 75p from HMSO

Woonerf, free from the Royal Dutch Touring Club ANWB, Wassenaarseweg 220, Postbus 2200, 's-Gravenhage, Netherlands

Controlling parking and access

Pedestrianisation schemes are generally welcome, but the signs that have proliferated to control access are too often ugly and confusing. The small but busy market town of Corsham (1) is an exception, finding that two small and discreet signs are all that is needed to keep out traffic (although the fact that the 'no vehicles' sign has been omitted on the left would seem to confirm that overall it is the appearance that keeps out vehicles, and not the signs). Probably the worst type of sign is that in central London (2): 'paved zone' is a phrase with no legal status, although the Department of Transport does insist on its use unless yellow lines are used to indicate 'no parking', but few drivers know this. The 'except for

access' is meant to apply only when lit, but can in fact be read at all times, and the whole sign is so large that it is completely out of scale with a pedestrian area. Other towns have tried different approaches: Ipswich (3) has remembered to ban cycling, but with a sign that requires concentration to interpret; Doncaster (4) uses a permissive rather than prohibitive sign; Hampstead, also in London (5) apparently removes its paving at 11.00 pm every night; while Ipswich (6) has another complicated sign that must be impossible for strangers to interpret without stopping. London's Leicester Square scheme also features this sign (7) as an alternative to its 'paved zone' ones.

Yellow lines to indicate parking restrictions look unpleasant and many suggestions have been made to replace this system of control, including reversing the system so that unlined streets would mean 'no parking' and lines would mean 'parking allowed' (when parked cars would often hide the lines anyway). The difference that yellow lines can make is shown by two cobbled streets in Durham (8 and 10). One solution has been achieved in Windsor (9) where the Department of Transport has allowed this sign to ban parking without yellow lines. But a similar approach in the Market Place at Durham (11) has had to be discontinued after pressure from the County Council and the police. Yellow lines have now reappeared in this historic area. Perhaps worst of all are double yellow lines in areas such as the entry point to a pedestrianised street in Colchester (12) and this narrow lane in Eton, near Windsor (13) where no driver ought even to consider parking.

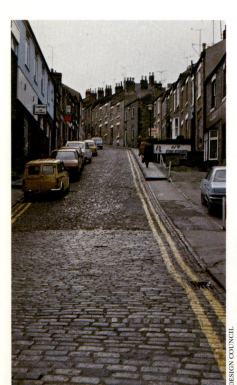

Shopfront design

by Candice Rodd, Design Council

Anyone whose exploration of our towns and cities was confined to their main shopping thoroughfares could be forgiven for concluding that British streets were produced from some mammoth kit of standard parts. Above shop level, the architecture may range widely and fascinatingly through the centuries; but, more often than not, what we actually *notice* is the same building society office, the same supermarket, the same chain store, duplicated almost infinitely throughout the land. Even small independent shops seem increasingly susceptible to the idea that generous expanses of glass and aluminium are the inevitable formula when designing their premises, regardless of the character of the original building.

While few would argue that the outward appearance of shops is a matter of widespread and urgent concern – especially compared with pressing issues like housing and traffic control – one local authority is sufficiently interested to have produced a document on the subject, part of an overall strategy to preserve and improve the local environment. Newbury's *Shop Front Design* guide, prepared jointly by the town's District Council and Berkshire County Planning Department, is not a list of rigid conservationist's rules, but a lively, well illustrated, sometimes controversial and self-confessedly subjective discussion of the whole subject. Its declared aim is to provide architects and developers with a strong indication of the approach the council is likely to take when considering planning applications for shop developments. To anyone interested in the appearance of our streets it offers telling illustration of how a little trouble and sensitivity on the part of planners could help reverse the seemingly relentless progress towards total uniformity, anonymity and mediocrity in our high streets.

Newbury itself is in many ways a typical English country town. Pretty but not picturesque, it lacks the grandeur of a Bath or York, but contains plenty of interesting Georgian and Victorian buildings, many of them listed, intermixed with a fair proportion of less inspiring contemporary architecture, such as the District Council's own modern brick offices. Although quite small, Newbury is an important shopping centre, so any attempts at preservation must be compatible with public and commercial demand for good, 'progressive' shopping facilities.

Contrasting approaches to shopfront design from two big building societies. (Above) the requirements of corporate image have not been allowed to ride roughshod over the premises' architectural integrity, but this subtle and sympathetic treatment nevertheless lets the Woolwich name come across. (Below) a much more typical approach, using the ubiquitous plate-glass and plastics formula which makes no concessions to its surroundings; this could be almost any shopping street in Britain.

Large areas of bright colour and plate glass no doubt ensure that shoppers notice Sherry's, but almost completely overwhelm the charm and character of this façade.

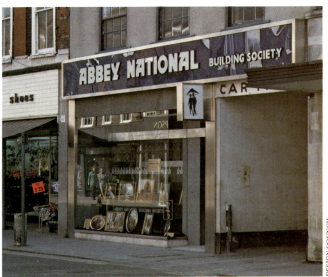

73

The approach exemplified in *Shop Front Design* is straightforward enough. Since the town contains a wealth of interesting architecture, the Council merely asks that shopfront developments should be in sympathy with the overall character of the buildings they occupy. Try putting that to the multiple retailers. The fact seems to be that, in any conflict between corporate identity and architectural discretion, corporate identity wins almost every time, presumably on the grounds that it is good for business. *Shop Front Design* argues that there need be no such conflict. Marks and Spencer is roundly condemned for the 'unacceptable and indiscriminate' application of house style in its Newbury branch, but the guide illustrates how, in the local offices of the Woolwich Building Society, the requirements of corporate image and conservation can be happily reconciled. About to occupy an attractive listed building, the Woolwich gave in gracefully to Council pressure, used timber instead of aluminium for the door and window frames, and even added perfect replicas of the surviving original pilasters to help restore the building's elegant appearance. The result is a frontage that enhances the local scene and can hardly do anything but good to the occupier's 'image'.

In case any developer should be innocent enough to suppose that a vaguely 'traditional' approach to shopfront design will automatically meet with Council approval and – more to the point – planning permission, the Newbury guide takes care to illustrate that a fine line exists between sensitive reproduction and 'ridiculous' pastiche – like the aluminium framed, bottle-glass, pseudo-Georgian frontage adopted by one well intentioned but confused shopfitter. The most pleasing and successful results, it claims, are achieved only when the building occupied is considered as an entity, with every shopfront detail designed to complement the whole.

One of the problems faced up to by the planners who produced the Newbury shopfront design guide is that the whole issue is intensely subjective. In an effort to ensure that the booklet would be of practical value, they have treated the subject under a number of useful headings. The question of contemporary design, for example, is discussed at some length. Here, where history supplies no models for faithful reproduction, the success or failure of a shopfront, both in its own right and in relation to its surroundings, is very much a matter of personal taste. Whether or not one personally likes all the examples chosen to illustrate 'good' contemporary shop design (few of them, incidentally, in Newbury itself; perhaps the town's historic nature is an inhibiting factor) it is hard to fault the guide's basic advice: modern designs should be bold, simple and interesting. While it may not always be feasible or even desirable to match a shopfront with the architecture above and alongside it, it is possible to avoid ludicrous juxtapositions of style.

Shop Front Design takes care to define what it calls a shop's 'changeable area' – that part of its frontage within which a proprietor can, up to a point, do what he likes, without serious detriment to the environment. A modern design, for example, can sometimes be successfully incorporated into an older building without detriment to the latter's proportions or to adjoining buildings, provided that alterations are restricted to the 'changeable' (basically door and window) area, leaving the 'balance' of the building intact.

Newbury may be unusual in its quantity of historic architecture, but even so, as in most urban areas, many of its shops are neither elegant period pieces nor bold statements of modern design, but modest enterprises housed in not particularly distinguished nineteenth and twentieth-century buildings. Since

Perhaps the shopfitter meant to demonstrate his versatility, but half-hearted and gratuitous attempts to recreate past styles rarely work. The Newbury guide urges a more sensitive and appropriate use of materials.

This exceptionally restrained Fine Fare frontage is in Chipping Campden, Gloucestershire. This treatment might not be appropriate to most shopping streets, but it does suggest that the usual brash supermarket formula is not compulsory or inevitable.

most proprietors probably have neither the cash nor the inclination to reconstruct their premises, the Council's policy here is to guard against thoughtless excesses, particularly in signs and advertisements, which can mar the appearance of a whole street. Disproportionately deep fascias, window stickers, inappropriate lettering, or even the use of too many, individually unexceptionable signs, can combine to destroy the character and architectural integrity of whole streets.

Where advertisements are concerned, local councils can invoke the support of legislation controlling their use when they constitute a threat to public safety or amenity. Since 'amenity' is defined as including the 'general characterisation of the locality, including the presence of historic, architectural or similar features of interest, these controlling powers are quite extensive. Yet it is significant that in *Shop Front Design*, notes about preventative legislation, though provided, occupy only a modest space at the end of the booklet. The guide's tone is far more one of encouragement, albeit didactic in places, than of big stick waving – a politic attitude in a subject so

IAN DAWSON

(Left) this exuberant façade more than holds its own against the British Home Stores standardised shopfront treatment. Alterations have been strictly confined to the lower part of the building and care has been taken to preserve or restore the architectural features of the upper storeys.

(Below left) an uncompromisingly modern shopfront, praised by the Newbury planners for its bold and simple use of materials. This kind of treatment can sometimes be incorporated in older buildings without a jarring clash of styles, provided that the shopfront designer respects the proportions of the original building and does not allow his installation to stray beyond what *Shop Front Design* calls the 'changeable area'.

(Below right) a pointed juxtaposition of styles. The rectangular illuminated sign is not inherently bad, but tends to be used indiscriminately, regardless of the character and period of the surroundings. Marks and Spencer's clock, in contrast, fits well with the style of the building and has enough individuality to make it a minor landmark.

BERKSHIRE COUNTY COUNCIL

DESIGN COUNCIL

The sameness of current shopfront designs tends to mask the architectural interest and variety of shopping streets, particularly in older towns. Here (this is Oxford) the effect is worsened by the use of over wide fascia panels which encroach upon the upper part of the facade and dominate the street.

(Below) a department store in Newbury's main shopping street. The shop's frontage follows the profile of the building and colour and lettering are restrained enough to complement rather than clash with the facade as a whole. In contrast, the electricity showroom (below right) seems crude and anonymous.

vulnerable to the vagaries of fashion and taste. It would be pointless, for example, to condemn outright the use of new materials like acrylics and aluminium, even in ancient Newbury, when these materials are widely available, relatively inexpensive, easy to maintain and long lasting. Instead the guide illustrates how, by the careful choice of colour, texture and finish, even seemingly brash and unsympathetic materials can be made to complement their surroundings.

How effective has *Shop Front Design* been so far in improving Newbury's street scene? The guide has sold steadily, if not like hot cakes, to architects and designers, and it has probably helped to persuade a few developers and proprietors to modify their plans for the better. It has not led to an overnight improvement in existing shopfronts and has so far proved ineffective in preventing the use of one of the Council planners' *bêtes noires*, the ubiquitous, boxy, standardised, projecting illuminated sign.

Has the booklet therefore been a worthwhile exercise? Chris Watts, of Newbury District Council's planning department, who was closely involved in preparing it, answers with a cautious yes, but admits a little ruefully that general lack of repair, especially of small, privately run shops, is still a bigger problem than shopfront design *per se*. Perhaps the guide's greatest value is in giving positive and tangible expression to constructive policies to improve the environment and in countering any assumption that the Council exists bureaucratically to impede progress rather than to encourage it. Also, in warning intending applicants of the kind of response they can expect when submitting proposals for planning permission, it may save a lot of time and irritation. As a tool for designers concerned about the urban environment and as an encouragement to thought and discussion about a widely neglected subject, its relevance extends far beyond Newbury.

Shop Front Design is available from Newbury District Council, Cheap Street, Newbury, Berkshire at £1.00 plus 15p postage.

Put out more flags

by Bob Kindred, Senior Planning Officer, Ipswich Borough Council.

DESIGN COUNCIL.

BOB KINDRED

BOB KINDRED

BOB KINDRED

BOB KINDRED

(Previous page) The Queen's Silver Jubilee in 1977 resulted in some rather tawdry banners in Trafalgar Square and elsewhere in London (top left) but little to compare with everyday American practice, shown by (top right) Broadway Plaza, Los Angeles, (bottom left) Rockefeller Centre, New York, (bottom right) Sansome Street, San Francisco, and (this page, above) Main Street, Hartford, Connecticut.

One would have thought that, since 1976 and 1977 were surely record years for flag manufacturers in the USA and the UK respectively, flags and banners would now be much more in evidence in our streets as a permanent reminder of how much more attractive our environment could be made to look. Once again the Americans have grasped ideas generated by their Bicentennial that have escaped us following the Jubilee. We should not have to wait until the Golden Jubilee before banners and flags reappear to brighten up our streets.

This sad state of affairs need not exist. Environmental graphic designers in America are turning to banners as an inexpensive but dynamic form of display to add colour and movement to the environment with the aid only of the sun and wind. The range of durable materials that is now available for both permanent and seasonal banners makes their use an attractive alternative to the plastic and neon uniformity of Main Street. The individuality of banners reflects a choice of materials which results from careful thinking about the image of businesses and the readability of signs. Many examples are appearing as a conscious reaction against the bland, repetitious, impersonal corporate images of large companies represented coast to coast. Locational and microclimatic considerations are, however, important when using cloth signs outdoors and it is clear that there will be situations in which flags and banners are not appropriate. Over-use would turn the idea into a cliché and devalue the principle behind it.

Cloth banners allow designers to produce signs, the textures and colours of which might be less acceptable in any other form, in such a way as to either complement a building or act as a foil for it. They also have the added advantage of being easily maintained or replaced. With the rapid and frequent changes in the images of our High Street shops, especially those selling clothes and footwear, this form of signing offers flexibility and variety. At the same time it creates a link with the products being sold by being constructed from similar materials. Buildings where the architectural detail does not suggest the use of conventional permanent signs, or small-scale spaces between buildings that would be overpowered by fixed illuminated signs, are particularly appropriate for 'soft' signing by banners.

Most of the American and Canadian cities that encourage imaginative signing give permission for flags and banners for periods of only one year in order to control the deterioration that might take place if the signs were exposed to long periods of extreme weather. It is interesting to note that cloth signs are promoted in cities such as Vancouver and Boston where climatic extremes are generally greater than anywhere in the United Kingdom.

Although cloth signs can be divided into types which reflect their function and location, they should not be categorised by designers before considering the requirements of their particular exterior or public interior application. Purely interior commercial signs in public spaces at the Broadway Plaza in Los Angeles are typical of the vertical paper signs that can be created without concern for the greater climatic wear and tear imparted on the cloth signs at Government Centre in Boston. While these signs are exposed to wind movement they are protected from the rain and snow by the pedestrian arcade. Where movement is a necessary adjunct to attract the attention of people it can be used to draw them into otherwise dreary or featureless alleyways and passages, catching the light in a way that no conventional fixed sign could do. This has been achieved particularly effectively in Boston and in San Francisco. Choice of colour is also important and can act either as a subtle counterpoint to existing building materials (brown banners and white lettering against soft brown brick in Ecker Street, San Francisco) or to attract attention (in pink, purple, orange and grey at an unobtrusive side entrance to Ghiradelli Square also in San Francisco). The growth of environmental information, urban interpretation trails and semi-permanent outdoor exhibitions has led to the use of banners applied cleverly to existing street furniture (and suitably designed to withstand strong winds) in vivid colours for easy identification at Hartford, Connecticut and in temporary structures such as a New York Bicentennial Exhibit to draw people into one of the out-of-the-way passages at Rockefeller Centre.

Will we see more banners here in Britain? It is to be hoped that designers will look more closely at using flags and banners in appropriate settings in future. The considerations which will influence designers are likely to be the relatively low cost and durability, flexibility of application and readability. The image of the client's business will be important and this may perhaps limit the use of cloth signs to small-scale, personalised businesses offering local specialist services which will be expressed in the individuality of each sign. One considerable influence on the final scheme may be the innate conservatism of planners when interpreting the Control of Advertising Regulations. There is growing concern by planners and the public alike about the visual quality of our streets and although planning controls have inhibited the grossest manifestations of inappropriate advertising they have not produced much positive visual interest or excitement. If flags and banners used carefully can be shown to work well, effectively and inexpensively in urban situations in the USA, and if this can be translated here, then this may be one way in which the advertising and signing of our environment can be improved.

Two more American examples, in this case advertising the Boston Repertory Theatre (top) and (right) various shops in the Government Centre, Cambridge Street, Boston. Both are more or less permanent installations and brighten up otherwise rather dreary surroundings.

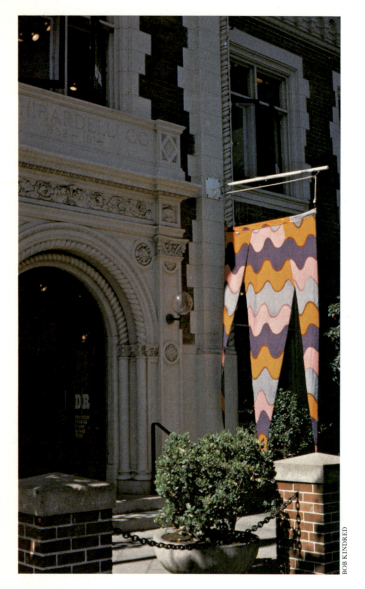

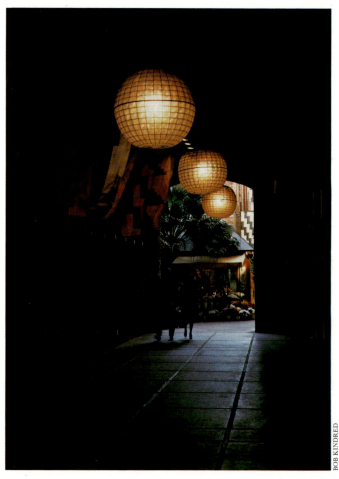

In flags and banners, as in some other fashions, San Francisco and the West Coast of America set the style, helped to some extent by the climate. These outdoor and indoor examples are from Ghiradelli Square (top left), Sansome Street (above), and Ecker Street, San Francisco (below) respectively.

Advertising in the environment

by Michael Middleton, Director, Civic Trust.

A society's attitude to outdoor advertising is coloured by two main, and separate, factors. The weight given to each is apt to change with the passage of time.

The first factor is a moral one. A developing, free-enterprise society tends to see all advertising as good and desirable in itself. By creating mass markets, the argument runs, advertising reduces the cost to the consumer of both goods and services. It thus constitutes the button that triggers the mainspring of an expanding economy and a constantly rising standard of living.

The opposite view is that large-scale advertising is a form of brainwashing, conditioning the public to desire and acquire material possessions for which it has no real need and which, in many cases, it is unable to afford. In this view, advertising contributes to a wholly materialistic view of life and, in so far as it tends constantly to push consumption upwards and thereby increase the exploitation of scarce resources, it is not in the longer-term interest of society.

This is not the place to debate such issues. Nonetheless it has to be recognised that, knowingly or unknowingly, individual responses to specific problems of outdoor advertising may be affected by these views and it seems necessary to record the fact at the outset.

The other main factor colouring society's attitude to outdoor advertising – and the one with which I am concerned – is the aesthetic one. It turns on the impact of posters and signs upon urban character and quality – in that horrid word used in planning legislation, 'amenity'. For more than half a century a running skirmish has swayed to and fro across this territory, conducted on the one hand by the outdoor advertising industry, on the other by the voluntary environmental societies and, latterly, local planning authorities.

The first Advertisement Regulation Acts dated from 1907 and 1925. It was with the Town and Country Planning Act of 1947, however, that central government really entered the fray as a kind of national umpire, setting out official rules for the game and, through the years since then, amending them from time to time. Currently, control of outdoor advertising is exercised in the interests of amenity or public safety in England and Wales by District Planning Authorities under Section 63 of the Town and Country Planning Act 1971 and the Control of Advertisements Regulations 1969, as amended by further Regulations in 1972 and 1974 made under that Act.

The broad effect of these Regulations is that certain classes of smaller and essentially functional signs are 'deemed' to have planning consent unless or until the planning authority objects to them; but that more conspicuous advertising, including most poster advertising, requires the planning authority's 'express consent' (normally limited to five years' duration). Planning authorities are further enabled to define 'Areas of Special Control', in which there is a general presumption against *all* advertising save the most innocuous and functionally necessary.

As a result of these 30 years of control, Britain has in fact tidied up the display of outdoor advertising to a point that is the envy of most other countries. No one who has seen the almost unbelievable free-for-all that obtains in North America and much of Europe can fail to be thankful for what has been achieved here at home. There are two notable plusses in particular. Over one third of Britain – mostly National Park land

The worst kind of outdoor advertising is ugly in itself and spoils an otherwise pleasant vista by its insensitivity. These skyline advertisements in Brussels (top) and Chicago (bottom) are particularly intrusive.

and open countryside – has been designated an Area of Special Control. We have thus been saved, almost entirely, the relentless proliferation of 48-sheet posters (or their equivalent) which hammer one from the verges and adjoining land of motorways and main roads in other countries. Second, we have avoided, with a handful of exceptions, that offensive proliferation of sky-signs with their obtrusive supports which so disfigure the buildings of most big cities abroad.

The part played by the industry itself in all this should not be overlooked; two initiatives in particular deserve mention. In the early 1960s, in an attempt to expand the design horizons of the industry itself and, through a more positive, design-conscious approach, to set up a constructive dialogue with architects and planners, the Poster Advertising Planning Committee was set up with James Adams, a Past President of both the Royal Planning Institute and the Institute of Landscape Architects, as its chief consultant. A useful – and still valid – booklet, *Posters Look to the Future*, was produced, suggesting ways in which outdoor advertising could be better integrated with its urban setting, and the PAPC undertook pilot projects to prove some of its points in Brighton and Killingworth.

At the same time the industry was beginning to introduce its new 4-sheet poster size, together with a variety of structures for its display. The seal of respectability was set on one of these – by London and Provincial – through a CoID Design Award in 1968, the first item of its kind to be thus recognised. The 4-sheet poster drum is now so accepted an element, in shopping areas and traffic-free precincts in particular, that it is hard to understand the opposition – or at least apathy – which the industry initially faced in making what was undoubtedly a real step forward.

So – how do things stand today? And what happens next? Well, there are powerful pressures to dismantle parts of the planning system as developed over the past 30 years – in part, as a matter of political precept to 'free the public from the stranglehold of an overweighted bureaucracy'; in part for economic reasons and, at least in theory, to streamline and speed up the planning process. Whether the moves so far proposed would have these effects is open to doubt. When a draft Government Order embodying a relaxation of the General Development Order was laid towards the end of 1977, the Association of District Councils claimed that its effect would be to *increase* the workload of planning authorities. In fact, the Government were defeated on this in the House of Lords and the Order was subsequently withdrawn from the Commons before debate.

Towards the end of 1976 a DoE Press Release announced the Government's intention, on economic grounds, to relax controls over certain types of outdoor advertising. In relation to poster advertising, a new 'deemed consent' was proposed permitting the display, for a maximum period of two years, of posters up to 48-sheet in size and not higher than 15 feet, covering one-third of the frontage or 30 metres if that be less, on hoardings surrounding construction sites in areas allocated in Development Plans for commercial or industrial purposes, other than in Conservation Areas. This, it may be noted, was a reversal of the Government's previously announced intention to *tighten up* control of outdoor advertising. (In fact, by mid-1978, the proposed revised Regulations had not been laid before Parliament and had consequently not come into effect.)

More control or less control? What is the role of poster advertising in the last quarter of the century? Perhaps it is time to state, and re-state-one or two basic principles.

The problem of poster advertising in urban areas can be divided into two parts: its introduction into existing settings, and its place in new development. The latter formed the main thrust of the PAPC campaign; it is the more easily dealt with and, in general, has been fairly satisfactorily handled over the past decade. However, the grandiose renewal schemes foreseen in the mid-1960s have by now disappeared from the drawing board. If only for financial reasons, more modest, make-do-and-mend schemes are now the order of the day – and are likely to remain so. The interface between poster display and the existing urban fabric thus seems to me the central issue which has to be grasped; it is this with which I shall concern myself in the remainder of this article.

The degree of acceptability of posters in existing settings must obviously depend upon the nature of the settings themselves. What is right for Shaftesbury Avenue is unlikely to be right for Parliament Square. *Posters Look to the Future* listed the following urban types with suggestions as to what forms of poster advertising might be appropriate to each: transport (railway stations and interchange points); central shopping districts; office areas; entertainment and cultural districts (I would raise an eyebrow myself about lumping together under such a heading, say, Piccadilly Circus and the South Kensington museums – but let it go); areas of sporting activity; industrial areas; and 'peripheral'.

Since this classification was suggested we have formalised our concern for certain types of area in a different way. We now have not only National Parks, Areas of Outstanding Natural Beauty and Heritage Coasts, but in addition some 5,000, mainly urban, Conservation Areas – of which 350 have so far been deemed 'Outstanding' by the Historic Buildings Council. Over 100 towns and cities are of sufficient architectural or historic importance to warrant effective 'Town Schemes' (ie are grant aided for conservation purposes jointly by central and local government).

It would now seem rational automatically to extend to all these the protection afforded by Section 63 (3) – the Areas of Special Control section – on grounds of amenity. Just to confuse the issue the Town and Country Amenities Act 1974 gives powers to the Secretary of State to make Regulations to control the display of advertisements in Conservation Areas. So far, however, no such Regulations have been made and it appears needlessly confusing to have – even potentially – two separate codes of control for use in Conservation Areas. Were Section 63 (3) to be applied to such areas, it would still be open of course to planning authorities to grant express consent for advertising within the terms of Regulation 27 (2) (b).

Here, lest it be thought that I am losing sight of the wider context, let me step back for a moment – as it were to refocus. Many elements combine to confuse and degrade the urban scene, apart from the quality of particular buildings, among them urban wasteland, unscreened car parks, overhead wires, traffic signing, poorly designed shopfronts, filling stations, advertising clutter and massed window stickers, illuminated signs, graffiti and litter. Poster advertising is sometimes, but by no means always or even generally, the most discordant of such notes. That does not absolve us from considering whether or not present relationships between poster displays and their context cannot be improved (while seeking no less to deal with the other problems I have indicated).

In brief, my own view is as follows:

1 By and large, 4-sheet posters and their display structures are acceptable and welcome in almost any commercial, shopping or transport concourse outside a Conservation Area, be the setting old or new; and may often be acceptable, if sensitively sited, in the shopping streets and pedestrian ways of Conservation Areas.

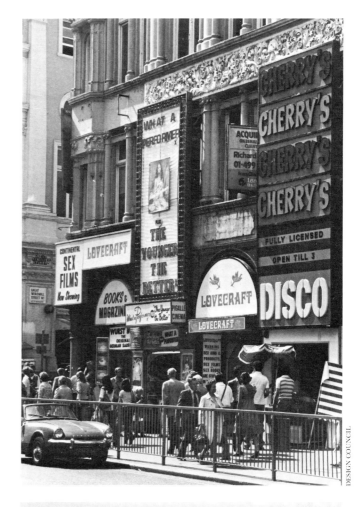

Traditionally, advertising has been a feature of London's Piccadilly Circus. But do these hoardings (top left) or shop signs (top right) really add anything to the vitality of the area? Hoardings in a residential area (bottom left) too often seem to be completely out of place, almost irrespective of the quality of the architecture. In contrast (bottom right) is the marvellous *trompe l'oeil* wall painting in Warrington, an advertisement that works well because it has been carefully designed to take advantage of its particular site.

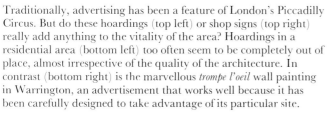

Posters can add colour and interest, but only if their presence is appropriate and the presentation well designed, as in this shopping precinct (bottom). But ill-kept sites in unsuitable surroundings (below) would be better replaced with something entirely different, in this case perhaps by trees and shrubs.

Hoardings are at their most harmful in areas where they loom over small-scale, attractive buildings. This pleasant cottage in the village of Woburn Sands (opposite page, top left) is completely spoiled by the adjacent hoardings (above).

The Grand Metropolitan High Stree

'The Grand Metropolitan High Street' (below) was the highlight of that company's annual report and well illustrates the appalling results that uncontrolled commercial pressures could bring to the street scene, with posters and signs plastered to almost everything with no regard to the quality of the buildings.

Roadside advertising signs, whether for temporary stalls or, as in this case (above) for a village shop, are not only ugly but can be distracting for drivers. At complex junctions (below) hoardings both unofficial and official add unnecessarily to the confusion of direction signs, although in this case the latter are hardly designed for clarity either.

2 Larger posters – ie 16 to 48-sheet – can happily be assimilated in appropriate types of new development, provided that planners, architects, designers and the industry work jointly to this end from the outset.
3 Larger posters - ie 16 to 48-sheet – are very difficult to relate to most existing urban settings, and should be prohibited totally in Conservation Areas.

Is there any need to spell out *why* larger poster are so disruptive in existing settings? There is the problem of scale. Only the largest settings can accept big posters comfortably; in the mean streets of an outworn nineteenth-century area their bright intrusiveness usually appears overpowering and arrogant. It is not easy to find appropriate spaces for free-standing structures; the flank walls and upper parts of buildings are therefore utilised, blacking out windows, blanketing architectural features, and destroying the unity of terraces originally conceived as a whole. The use of hoardings surrounding disused land disguises the fact that such land is awaiting fuller use; sites like the notorious South Kensington triangle, originally earmarked for the National Theatre, have been surrounded by posters for decades on end. Large poster stations at traffic junctions and roundabouts are apt to confuse the informational signals sought by the driver and can sometimes be faulted on safety grounds. Finally – and it is sad to have to say it – there is the question of poster design as such. Forget the old line about posters being the poor man's art gallery and the only art form with which the public is in daily contact. It had a grain of truth 40 years back when a new Kauffer design or a Cassandre or a Graham Sutherland was an event; there is no formal quality in a large photograph of a frying sausage which relates in any way to what is generally meant by the word art.

Could it be – I pose the question in a genuine spirit of enquiry – that the larger poster, in its traditional form, has had its day and in 15 or so years' time will be as extinct as the dodo? I am not suggesting that large displays will cease to exist. As I have already stated, certain types of new development in particular can provide very suitable settings; it could be, however, that these will be painted posters, individually tailored to their individual settings, rather than printed 48-sheet posters looking for a flat surface on which to come to rest.

In short, it is perhaps time for another re-adjustment by the industry, to carry forward the ideas initiated in the mid-1960s. Without accepting the rather desperate suggestion implied by *Posters Look to the Future* that the city is going to be so vast and so impersonal that only outdoor advertising can humanise it, we all know that advertising of the right sort in the right place enlivens the street scene and that without it – as in the towns of Eastern Europe – places can appear very dead indeed. Positive approaches are needed and a new set of design guidelines, agreed by the outdoor advertising industry and the planning authorities, would do much to reconcile the interests of the industry with today's ideas about conservation and rehabilitation, which are so different from the James Adams vision of large-scale urban redevelopment. Such guidelines would speed up the planning process and save staff time because everyone concerned would be more confident about just what was permissible and what not. West Sussex issued a very clear-cut guide some years ago, and there is no reason why its example should not be developed more fully on a national basis. For in the last analysis the best answers, as always in these matters, will emerge only through sensitivity to the visual proprieties and through the creative eye of the designer.

The most frequent excuse for hoardings is that they disguise an ugly vacant site. This has been said about these hoardings opposite London's Victoria and Albert Museum (below), but the site has been empty for many years, and a small garden would be more appropriate.

Good outdoor advertising means matching design with the environment as with this group of shop signs in Cambridge (below). The 'Keep Britain Tidy' sticker (bottom) can itself become a nuisance when applied without thought to every lamp-post, bollard and fence.

Parks for pleasure

MARY MITCHELL

MARY MITCHELL

Pleasant parks can be created out of derelict areas. The lake and surrounding area at Camp Hill in Nuneaton, Warwickshire, was overgrown and full of rubbish, with the lake itself silted up and weedy. An improvement scheme, partly aimed at making the area safe after a fatal accident, has created a place where children can find much of interest and where adults can relax.

The play area includes (above left) slides running down a natural slope into a sandpit and a large paddling pool, with toilets and the filtration plant moulded into the hillside. The lake itself (above right) has been dredged and the banks remodelled and contained by natural timber piles. The rough paving surround adds to safety by inhibiting slipping when wet, and the seats are made from local split logs. Designer Mary Mitchell is keen on using local materials, and this old oak (below) provides a natural 'sculpture' and an interesting place for kids.

MARY MITCHELL

Trees, shrubs, flowers and grass can brighten almost any area and are essential in humanising what would otherwise be unpleasantly hard surroundings. Many new shopping precincts, such as that in Blackburn (top left), have planting as in integral part of the design. But planting can also break up the wide expanse of an old street that has been pedestrianised, as in Hereford (above right). This pleasant pond (left) is in the centre of the Surrey village of Lingfield, while Woburn Walk in London is made still more attractive by its trees and flowers. City centre roundabouts are usually tarmac monstrosities or simply grassed areas with a few small flowers that look rather sad in their unnatural surroundings. Bristol (bottom left) has solved the problem with trees and large shrubs that are in scale with the buildings and vehicles. The colours of trees and shrubs demand care in choosing the colour of the man-made objects in parks. These sky-blue benches in Victoria park in London are an eyesore compared with their muted neighbours.

City centre planting can take many forms. This vacant building site in central London (top left) has been turned into a pleasant Japanese-style garden, while this street in Bath (top right) uses hanging baskets to good effect.

Such prettifying would be out of place in more rugged areas, but even here much can often be done to improve the environment. Darwen Robin Bank near Blackburn was littered with the signs of industrial dereliction (bottom left) before being cleaned up. The river wall was rebuilt, unnecessary street furniture removed, and the whole hillside was remodelled using thousands of tons of free topsoil, partly to accommodate a 115-foot long zig-zag slide (bottom right).

Rural areas can be as neglected as urban sites. The Cumbrian village of Bouth was stirred into action by a proposal to build on an empty central site. Following protest meetings, the land (top right) was handed into the trusteeship of the Parish Council and a plan for a new village green and play area was designed and approved. All the work was done over two years by voluntary Sunday working-parties of villagers, one result being that village pride has since maintained the area in excellent condition (above). Bouth won the 'Best Kept Small Village in Cumbria' award in 1976. The judges commented, 'A vast amount of communal and corporate pride has gone into this village. The centre of the village is neat and litter-free, the children's play area was a delight . . . it was the only clean telephone box I met'.

Queen's Park in Blackburn uses local secondhand materials including road kerbs and setts and stone from the floors of demolished mills (top left). The stream is a major feature and is surfaced in York stone setts to protect the main water supply (centre left). As usual with Mary Mitchell's parks, the ground modelling is vital (bottom).

A disused sewage works hardly sounds like the ideal site for a play centre for children, but that is what the Markfield park in the London borough of Haringey used to be. The concrete treatment bays have been retained (right), forming an ideal area for sand play, with climbing frames, seats for parents, and gaps in the walls for access being left unfinished to add to the air of informality and adventure that small children enjoy.

The grounds of a children's hospital can be useful in helping kids get better, but are too often uninteresting or just overgrown. The Royal Liverpool Children's hospital makes the best of its grounds and has been fortunate in obtaining an old fire engine, lifeboat and aircraft (below and below right) as popular playthings.

The Dumbleton Copse playground in Southampton was designed as a focal point for children and their parents in a new estate that was cut off from the main part of the city. The playground uses wood from trees cleared when opening up the copse, and depends as much on ground modelling as on formal equipment for its effectiveness. It was largely paid for by voluntary fund raising.

Gable end murals can enliven drab areas: this Swindon car park (1)
is an excellent example. The murals, designed by the Thamesdown
Community Arts Project all reflect local life, the locomotive relating
to Swindon's history as a railway centre and the canal-side scene (0)
shows what life in this particular area used to be like. Most show-
cases are comparatively small, but this giant (2) provides the
centrepiece for Bolton's pedestrian area: it houses an old steam
engine. Water can always provide an attractive feature: the
bollards, trees, and surfacing make the best of this lock at
Georgetown, Washington DC (3).

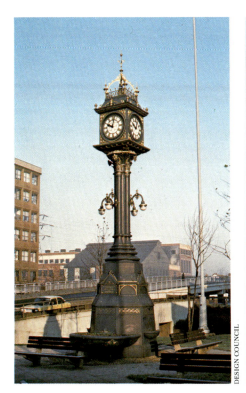

Traditionally, clocks, statues, fountains and town name-signs have all provided decorative centrepieces in towns and villages. The old clock in Rotherham (4) has been beautifully cleaned and re-painted, while the concrete decoration in Brighton's Churchill Square (5) and the stainless steel sculpture at the Embarcadero Centre in San Francisco (6) are both unashamedly modern. The traditional sign in Southwold, Suffolk (7), was painted for the 1977 Silver Jubilee. The fountain and mosaic (8) are in the First National Bank of Chicago Plaza, Chicago.

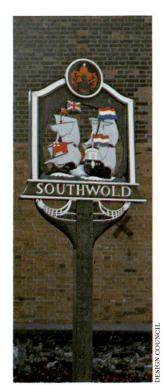

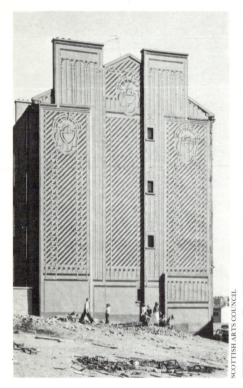

SCOTTISH ARTS COUNCIL

DESIGN COUNCIL

Decorative features can be used to improve otherwise drab walls or buildings, or they can simply be visual centrepieces with no other function. The gable end mural in Ancroft Street in the Maryhill district of Glasgow (9) won a Scottish Arts Council award for its designer Tim Armstrong; it is in red and black on a green background. Also disguising a blank wall – in this case vacant shops units adjacent to Westminster Cathedral in London (10) – are these attractive scenes from historic London. Bus shelters can rarely be described as decorative, but this new one in Enham Alamein in Hampshire (11) uses local materials and provides an interesting feature on the village green. The modern sculpture outside Orchestra Hall in Minneapolis (12) is the modern equivalent of the statues that traditionally formed the centrepiece in town squares.

The Swindon murals are designed by the Thamesdown Community Arts Project and reflect local life: the locomotive (1 on page 92) relates to the town's history as a railway centre, while the canal-side scene (opposite) commemorates the local poet Alfred Williams.

DESIGN COUNCIL

MINNEAPOLIS CONVENTION AND TOURISM COMMISSION

Graffiti are normally a problem in pedestrian subways. Not so in Glenrothes, a New Town in Scotland, where local schoolchildren produced this mural.

Children's playgrounds: safe or sorry?

by Paul Burall, Design Council

Mark Jolly was only six years old when he was killed by a climbing frame which fell on him in a Scottish playground: three days before the accident, the local Council had been warned that the frame was unsafe, but had done nothing. A Midlands girl was badly injured when part of the metal surface of a slide entered her leg just below the knee and gouged through to the top of her thigh. An 11-year-old Newcastle girl broke her ankle when she put her foot through a gap left by a missing plank on a roundabout: the local Council was told about the fault but did nothing for more than two weeks, during which time the damaged roundabout had injured four more children. In Wapping, a 60-year-old heavy iron rocking-horse which rears some 1.5 metres into the air and crashes down to within 100mm of the ground remains in use, despite having injured numerous London children over the years and despite the local Council having been forced to pay £4,500 High Court damages to one of the victims. Steven Porritt, a Yorkshire four-year-old, was lucky: he suffered only a broken jaw after falling through a 300mm-wide gap at the top of a slide 3.5 metres high; in another accident involving a fall from a slide a seven-year-old Twickenham girl died. Mark Jennings, aged 13, also died after being thrown from a pendulum swing in Keynsham. A Yorkshire seven-year-old was killed falling from a school climbing frame onto tarmac. . .

These are just a few of the individual tragedies that make up an alarming total of accidents that occur in children's playgrounds each year. Surveys carried out by the Design Council indicate that at least 20,000 children are taken to hospital in Britain annually for treatment following accidents involving playground equipment in public parks and play areas; many more such injuries are treated by local doctors or at home. And a recently completed three-year study at London's University College Hospital suggests that one to two per cent of all childhood hospital admissions are caused by accidents in playgrounds and that such accidents account for some four per cent of all accidents involving the hospital admission of a child.

The problem is by no means unique to Britain. The American National Recreation and Park Association has analysed many accidents as part of its work on a Safety Standard for Public Playground Equipment, and the Standards Association of Australia has estimated that more than 60,000 children are injured each year in playgrounds in Australia.

There is, of course, no such thing as a totally safe playground. Children need adventure and look for challenge: a playground which offers neither will soon be deserted by

children who may well instead be attracted to play by canals, railways, in derelict buildings, or on the roads, all of which are likely to be more dangerous than any playground. Nevertheless, too many playground injuries are unnecessary. Poor maintenance, bad design and ill thought-out siting all cause accidents without adding anything to the attractions of a playground. Indeed, some of the safer innovations introduced recently into playgrounds for safety reasons also have greater potential for excitement than the older, less safe, items they replace.

Injuries involving falls

Both the University College Hospital study and an earlier survey carried out at the Sheffield Children's Hospital indicate that the great majority of the more severe injuries occurring in playgrounds result from falls. In the London study, falls from climbing frames accounted for 30 per cent of the hospital admissions, despite the fact that other surveys have shown that climbing frames are not particularly popular with children and, on average, are used for less than 10 per cent of the total time spent by each child on playground equipment.

Such injuries can be prevented or made less severe in two ways. First, the height from which a child can fall can be minimised. In the case of slides, all except the very smallest should be placed down the natural slope of a mound or a playhouse roof so that it is impossible to fall vertically for any distance. This not only eliminates the deaths and severe injuries caused by children falling from traditional tower slides, but it creates opportunities for very long slides following the contours of a hill and incorporating curves, which children find much more enjoyable. Again, climbing frames should be limited in height: the new British Standard is laying down a maximum height from which free fall is possible of 2.5 metres, although this is inevitably a compromise since a fall of one metre or even less can cause injury.

So the second measure to help mitigate a fall is to provide a surface under climbing equipment and slides which will absorb the energy of a child falling without causing severe injury. Considerable work is going on investigating different kinds of

Two of the most dangerous types of equipment are the plank swing (below left) and the ocean wave (below right). The frequency of accidents on such equipment is not necessarily high, but the combination of speed of movement and extreme weight can cause very severe injuries.

safety surface, but no ideal surface combining the qualities of being maintenance free, economic, weather resistant and safe has yet been found. Nevertheless there are several materials that are so much safer than the usual concrete, tarmac, or hard-packed earth that their minor disadvantages should not prevent them being used under equipment from which children may fall.

Several types of specially made rubber surface are now available, usually with a cellular construction to assist energy absorption. Experience has shown such surfaces to be durable and weather resistant, but they are expensive to install, although this may be balanced by low maintenance costs. Natural materials are initially cheaper, but require regular maintenance and may only be suitable in supervised playgrounds where dogs and petty vandalism can be controlled. Of these natural materials, pea gravel is probably the best. A bed of pea gravel to a depth of about 200mm absorbs impact energy satisfactorily and drains well, but requires regular raking to maintain the depth and can be thrown about: it has the benefit of being relatively easy to walk on yet discourages running or cycling. Wood chips absorb energy extremely well but retain moisture and rot, while pine bark and similar materials are also satisfactory in terms of energy absorption but are not particularly durable. Sand to a depth of 250mm can be satisfactory if it is of a type that does not bind tightly, but it does require regular raking; hard-packed sand is not satisfactory.

There are other danger points with slides and climbing frames. The surface of a slide should be constructed from one continuous strip of metal, as jointed strips have been known to come apart and the joints themselves have sometimes tempted vandals to insert nails or razor blades between the sections, with nasty results. It is also obviously important to avoid any projections or sharp edges on both climbing frames and slides.

Moving equipment

Perhaps the biggest improvement in playground safety since

The swing seat (below) had been in use for several months before action was taken to remove the obvious danger. Less obvious than the broken bolt are the severely worn chain links, which could easily break without warning.

This new playground (below) demonstrates many of the dangers facing children. The swing seats have hard edges that emphasise any impact; the barriers are ideal for sitting on and sited so that kids jumping off the swings may well collide with children jumping the barrier; and the tarmac surface does nothing to soften falls.

the Design Council launched its campaign to reduce playground accidents in 1972 is likely to result from the introduction of the new British Standard for Permanently Installed Outdoor Play Equipment. Unlike the Standard it replaces, this recognises that good playground equipment should stimulate children's imagination and that it must therefore be reasonably safe however it is used. Thus the traditional excuse that accidents are caused by children 'misusing' equipment has been repudiated: by definition, a child cannot 'misuse' play equipment. The second major change in the new Standard is that it frees designers and manufacturers from tight descriptive specifications and instead imposes certain minimum performance standards covering such aspects as strength, endurance, and the maximum impact load which equipment should be able to inflict on a child.

The new Standard sets the maximum impact load at 50 times the force of gravity ($50g$), a force which can still cause concussion. This will drastically change the appearance of many playgrounds, for several existing types of equipment are so far outside the $50g$ limit that they ought to disappear, not just from manufacturers' lists, but also from all playgrounds. Two items in particular are so heavy and dangerous that responsible local authorities are already removing them. These are the plank swing and the ocean wave (also known as the witch's hat), both of which are intrinsically heavy and, especially when loaded with four or five children, can deliver a lethal blow to anyone getting in their path. They both rely on braking or restraining mechanisms that have proved not to be fail-safe, and this in itself can make them extremely dangerous. Pendulum swings suffer from much the same defects.

Ordinary single swings can be dangerous too, but the risk of severe injury can be reduced considerably by replacing hard-edged wood or plastics seats with a seat that will spread or absorb an impact load. Special safety seats – usually using a cellular rubber construction – are now available, and old car tyres achieve the same result and have the added advantage that children seem to prefer their informality.

Other kinds of moving equipment present different problems. Rocking-horses cause a number of quite serious injuries each year, usually when a child's knee or leg is crushed by the descending horse: the new British Standard requires rocking-horses to be designed to brush aside a child without crushing whichever part of the body is in the way. Any horse which fails to meet this requirement, or whose weight and potential speed could cause an impact greater than $50g$, is intrinsically danger-

ous, which means that most existing rocking-horses ought to be scrapped. The major problem with roundabouts is caused by older children pushing them too fast so that younger children are either thrown off or jump off in fright; fail-safe speed control systems are therefore essential, and the use of a safety surface also helps. Major injuries resulting from a child falling under a roundabout are less likely with smaller, lighter types. See-saws should also incorporate fail-safe mechanisms to prevent them from coming too close to the ground and crushing children's feet and also a braking mechanism to ensure that the speed of the reversal of direction is gradual rather than sudden.

Siting

The way in which playgrounds are laid out can have an important effect on safety. All moving equipment should be sited away from the natural path of children running between items or into and out of the playground. Equipment for younger children should be placed away from areas likely to attract the bigger children and should preferably be close to seats where parents can sit and supervise. If possible, dogs and bicycles should be kept out of playgrounds, as both can be the cause of accidents.

Barriers and fences need treating with great care. If used at

Many accidents to children in playgrounds are caused by a lack of thought. The 'barrel walk' (below) operates like a giant hamster wheel, and a number of accidents have occurred when children's fingers have become trapped in the slots. The manufacturer blames the children for putting their fingers through the slots – an excuse that typifies the view that playground accidents are usually caused by 'misuse'. But can children 'misuse' equipment that ought to be designed to stimulate their imagination and test their physical skills? The new British Standard states clearly that equipment must be reasonably safe, however it is used.

Poor standards of maintenance are a frequent cause of accidents. Sometimes faults are obvious (below right) and there can be no excuse for such damage not being spotted and repaired promptly. But underground corrosion (bottom right) resulting in the sudden and unexpected collapse of equipment is more difficult to check. The Greater London Council inspects the underground support of its playground equipment every five to seven years by digging away the surface to carry out visual and other tests.

WAKEFIELD EXPRESS SERIES LTD

DESIGN COUNCIL

DESIGN COUNCIL

all, they should be designed so that children cannot sit on them or treat them as climbing frames. The detailed positioning of fences requires considerable thought if they are to function correctly in preventing children from getting into the path of moving equipment without themselves becoming a trap, for instance, for anyone jumping from a swing. Perhaps the best advice is to make sure that someone with experience of children's play and playgrounds is consulted about every aspect of the design of a new playground.

Maintenance

While thoughtless siting and poor equipment contribute substantially to accidents and injuries, bad maintenance is also a regular culprit. Problems range from the unexpected collapse of equipment as a result of corrosion or other defects, which develop over a long period of time, to damage caused by day-to-day wear and vandalism. The former is the more insidious because it can lead to a major tragedy with no warning, and the Great London Council is now carrying out tests on all its equipment at five-year intervals in order to spot defects before they become serious. The inspections include breaking up the surfaces around tube supports to see whether they have corroded below ground level. This visual inspection, backed by tests with a hammer, is followed up by non-destructive testing using ultrasonic or fibre optic equipment. Clamping bolts securing tripod castings and shackle clamps on horizontal bars have been found to be susceptible to corrosion, especially in crevices between clamped components. These weaknesses can usually be spotted visually, as can the brittle fractures that occur in iron castings.

Some of the risks from these hidden defects can be avoided. Support tubes, for example, should be embedded in concrete rather than asphalt and the surface should be contoured to shed water. Some equipment is now being made so that the supports can be released from special below-ground sockets so that the underground support tubes can be inspected easily. Components that are known to wear, such as swing chains, should be strong enough to last for the whole life of the equipment, thus reducing risks if inspections are missed.

The least defensible accidents are those caused by obvious defects which have not been repaired. There are many cases on the Design Council's files of accidents involving equipment left in a dangerous state for days and weeks after being reported as faulty. Even when action is taken, lack of thought can cause a tragedy. One council removed a faulty climbing frame from a park to an adjacent maintenance area where an 11-year-old boy found it, started to climb, and caused it to fall on him, resulting in a serious back injury: there was no fence between the playground and the maintenance area.

All play equipment ought to be inspected visually every day to check that vandals have not removed bolts, broken boards on the roundabout, or sabotaged the slide. A more thorough visual inspection should be made at, say, monthly intervals to check against rotting boards, damaged steps, and similar defects. Provided that the person carrying out the inspection is told what to look for, these checks do not require special skills or tools. Full-scale technical checks either by the manufacturer or another qualified person should be carried out annually.

Careful choice of equipment, an understanding of how children behave, and detailed attention to inspection and maintenance can ensure that a playground is attractive and stimulating without putting children unnecessarily at risk of serious injury.

Two excellent playgrounds that combine the essentials of safety and excitement are at Warrington (above) and Blackburn (below). The Warrington playground is covered with a thick layer of 'Leca' lightweight aggregate that cushions falls and is kept in place by being set well below the surrounding path; the swings have old tyres as safety seats, and the slide is designed so that kids cannot fall vertically. The Blackburn slide is also safer that the usual tower slide because it eliminates the risk of long falls; its 120-foot length and curves are also more appealing.

Skateboarding: passing fad or new boom sport?

by Hywel Griffiths, The Sports Council.

The recent boom in the sport of skateboarding has made it the *bête noire* of many local authorities. Pressure to provide facilities is being put upon authorities by the skateboarders themselves, who are claiming that their sport has as much right to facilities as any other; by parents and other adults concerned about the safety of children skateboarding on pavements or footpaths where they could come into disastrous contact with cars or pedestrians; and by the police, who are becoming increasingly worried about both safety and the need to enforce the law (so far they have in most cases turned a blind eye to the possible illegality of pavement skating).

Balancing these moral and sporting needs is the understandable reluctance of authorities to spend large sums on a sport which may turn out to be a passing fad. However, the high initial capital cost of skateboards and safety equipment, together with the boom in the formation of clubs and the arrival of a national Skateboard Association and possibly a proper competitive structure, suggest that the activity will consolidate into a sport with a well defined core of support.

What can local authorities and others do to meet this dilemma? First, it must be realised that skateboarding facilities can be provided in a number of ways and that the large and expensive concrete skatepark is at the top end of the scale. A hierarchy of skateboarding areas might include a local non-specialist area, a small purpose-built facility, a large skatepark, and finally an indoor skatepark, each of which will have its own individual characteristics and requirements, advantages and disadvantages, and will provide particular challenges and experiences for the skateboarder. The following paragraphs describe these types and their requirements.

The local non-specialist area is the smallest and the least expensive facility and can be provided in a wide variety of locations for the use of small groups of participants. It can include a flat, slightly inclined, or undulating surface which must be smooth, but may not have been specially designed for skateboarding. A number of existing areas can be adapted to make them suitable. These include school playgrounds, hard tennis courts, empty paddling, boating or swimming pools, paths or hard slopes in parks, kick-about areas, roller skating rinks and, indoors, in sports halls and disused buildings. Such areas can be adapted by the provision of ramps for the performance of the 'kick turn' – a technique essential for progression to the more advanced manoeuvres on more difficult facilities. Ramps can be made of wood with marine plywood faces or they can be metal structures with aluminium or polymeric faces and may be either permanently fixed or demountable. Such areas provide a capacity of approximately one skater per 10 square metres and require only casual and intermittent supervision. Warning signs to pedestrians and possibly notice boards for clubs using a particular site are required. First aid facilities should be easily available and there are many advantages in ensuring that clubs develop on the site, giving a better degree of control or supervision.

A small specialist area can serve a whole borough or small town and should provide at least one freestyle area as described above, preferably with a surface specially provided for skateboarding and with fixed 'kick turn' ramps. It should also have at least one specialist 'skate run' (these are described below). Such a facility would require control and supervision and a small charge might be made. The park would need to be divided according to skill to prevent beginners moving on to the more advanced 'runs' before they are ready. Small specialist parks can be provided using modular and free-standing units. A number of firms have produced ramps, 'quarter pipes', 'half pipes', 'full pipes' and 'bowls' in the form of pre-cast plastics, glass fibre or glass reinforced concrete sections. While no such parks exist in the UK at the time of writing they can be a fast and effective way of providing smaller facilities. They are at the moment relatively expensive, but price movements will depend upon demand. Ramps have been described above, but 'quarter pipes', 'half pipes' and 'full pipes' may be new terms to the reader. They have developed, along with much of the other skateboarding patois, from the American scene where large land drainage and sewerage pipes were used by skateboarders. The 'full pipe' is a full circle of two metres radius or more and two to three metres in length, which the skater uses in a rocking motion to get as high up the side of the pipe as gravity and his accumulated speed will allow. A 'half pipe' is the lower section and the 'quarter pipe' one half of this; 'quarter' and 'half' pipes usually need to be supported or sunk into the ground and all may be constructed of materials other than concrete piping.

Large specialist areas are known as skateparks and these consist of a freestyle area, as described above, plus a number of freestanding pipes or bowls and a number of skate runs. Such parks require high standards of design and supervision to combine safety with excitement for the participants. The planning and management aspects that need to be considered are safety, liability, internal control and supervision, visibility, first aid, floodlighting, geology and drainage, planning and building regulations. These are covered in greater detail in TUS Data Sheet 19 (see page 105).

Skate runs are the more advanced facilities for skateboarding. They include slaloms, bowls, snakes and a number of hybrids of these basic types. Downhill slalom runs are inclined plane surfaces with a flat start area at the top and a run out area which may be flat or dished at the end. Cones are placed on the slope and the skateboarder has to weave his way in and out of the cones in the fastest time. The slope is normally a minimum of seven metres wide to allow two lanes and 50 metres would be a reasonable distance for competition (100 metres is common in the USA, but the Skateboard Association in the UK have not as yet announced competitive distances for downhill slalom). The slopes will vary in angle, but between $3°$ and $10°$ will be suitable (steeper angles for shorter runs). The Skateboard Association's rules cover only ramp start and push start slaloms, both of which can be performed on flat areas.

Bowls may be of two types: open bowls and 'performance' or 'drop' bowls. Open bowls are larger, have gentler slopes and only part of the bowl is used in any one ride. 'Performance' or 'drop' bowls are smaller, steeper and deeper. The nearest equivalent is a fairground wall of death ride where the rider uses his acceleration to overcome the gravitational forces as he rides around the rim of the bowl. If properly designed such a facility will not be dangerous for skilled skateboarders. Such a bowl consists of four basic elements:

1 A collection area where skaters await their turn to start. This should be narrow enough to encourage orderly queueing and also provide clear views of the whole of the rest of the run to avoid collision.

2 An entry ramp where the skater gains speed. This should be wide enough to allow only one skater at a time (two to three metres) and may be flat or dished. Gradients should not exceed $30°$ and the entry should be at either the middle or the edge of the bowl.

3 The bowl, the diameter of which will vary according to the length and steepness of the slope, with walls not exceeding 4 metres in height, with the highest point opposite the point of entry. The angle of the walls will vary with the steepest point

opposite the point of entry, the bottom will be flat or dished, and the walls should rise in a concave slope. Angles will vary between 60° and 80° at the steepest point.

4 The point of exit, which will vary according to the shape of the bowl, but steps or hand holds should be discouraged. However, skaters should be able to leave the bowl without causing a hazard to others.

The advice of a consultant skilled in skatepark design is strongly recommended before such a facility is contemplated.

'Snake' runs are similar to bobsleigh runs, but without the ice. The run is sinuous in long profile with a concave curved cross section. The outsides of the curves are banked and the skater at the top should, so far as possible, be able to see the whole run before starting. The length of the run will depend upon the space available; a longer run may be produced by curving the run back upon itself. Slopes should not exceed 5° as the excitement of the run is achieved by swaying back and forth up the walls of the channels. The radius of the curve and the height and angle of the banking are all inter-related and the services of a skilled consultant are recommended before designing such a facility.

It is likely that skateparks in the UK will be smaller than many of the vast parks built in the USA, and particularly in California, and the layout of the runs and the need for control points therefore more important here. There are on sale a number of manuals that claim to provide all the design information necessary to build skateparks. While these can be valuable they should be approached with some caution as they are almost all derived from the USA where conditions, particularly related to layout, climate and costs, vary considerably from those in Britain.

The fourth type of facility is the indoor skatepark. This is a peculiarly British development brought about by the rigours of our climate. Indoor facilities can be provided in one of three ways.

First, by simple adaptation of existing spaces, in sports halls for example, by the addition of ramps. There is no information currently available on the effect of skateboard wheels on floors, but provided that a suitable floor seal is used there should be no ill effects. Seals recommended for roller skating by the National Skating Association are suggested.

Second, outdoor skateparks can be covered by demountable structures such as air halls or geodetic structures of fabric-clad aluminium. Such parks will have greater restrictions on numbers due to the regulations on means of escape, but there are examples in the UK which seem to work successfully.

Third, large redundant buildings with an open floor plan such as warehouses, churches, cinemas and aircraft hangers can be made into skateparks either by the simple addition of wooden ramps to existing floors or by the use of modular units. Heavy materials such as sprayed or plastics reinforced concrete should be used with care due to problems of load bearing in some buildings.

Having discussed what kind of facilities might be provided, it is appropriate to consider who should provide them and how they should be provided. The main options are, first, direct provision by a local authority or by private enterprise or, second, joint ventures between the two.

Almost all the local non-specialist facilities will be provided by local authorities or by skateboard clubs. It must be understood, however, that having made such a provision the local authority must not think that it has completely discharged its responsibility. By making basic sites available skateboarders will be encouraged to improve and test their skills under more demanding conditions and unless the skaters are going to be

Large, specialist areas known as 'skateparks', like the one at Fordham Park, New Cross, South London (above) are a fairly expensive way of providing facilities for all types of skateboarding. Less ambitious schemes can be built up from smaller units, such as this marine-ply ramp at Croydon Skatepark.

driven back to the dangers of the pavements and the roads, more advanced facilities are going to be needed. The majority of the small, purpose-built facilities will also be provided by local authorities and voluntary organisations. It is unlikely that skateboard clubs will be able to raise the capital to provide such facilities themselves, but they could play an important part in assisting with design and management, thus reducing operating costs for the sponsoring body.

The larger skateparks will be provided more equally by investment of commercial and public funds or by a combination of the two. The Skateboard Association maintains a list of designers and constructors of skateparks and this list also covers firms that offer joint management arrangements.

In the wake of some fairly unsatisfactory, but highly damning, tests on skateboards by *Which?* magazine and the general absence of design guidance for facilities, a Trade Association known as the British Skateboard Trade Council has been set up to monitor standards within the industry, both for boards and for facilities. One of its early tasks will, it is hoped, be to approach the British Standards Institute for a 'Kitemark' for skateboards.

One of the more complex current skateboarding debates is that of what type of surface should be provided. Traditionally, at least in the USA, skateparks have been built in concrete and the complex geometric forms involved have meant that sprayed concrete is the most commonly used technique. Its other advantage is that the spraying technique produces a stippled surface which gives excellent traction for the urethane wheels of the skateboard. Both the 'Gunite' and 'Shotcrete' techniques of spraying concrete have been used successfully and the Cement and Concrete Association recommend a sprayed concrete meeting BS 5328:1976 as suitable for skate-board facilities (for more information on concrete surfaces see *The Surveyor* 13 April 1978).

In the UK certain alternative materials have been suggested for skatepark surfaces and, while there is little information available at the time of writing, each can be considered on its merits. These materials are:

1 Glass reinforced concrete in modular units
2 Glass reinforced polymers in modular units
3 Some types of asphalt – only suitable for flat or gently sloping areas
4 Timber – either as fixed or demountable ramps or formed into bowls or runs
5 Rubber – sheet rubber has been used on natural contours
6 Metal – preformed for bowls or runs or for ramps
7 Tile – plastic or mineral tiles in existing dry pools or laid directly on to natural contours.

Finally, to understand the skateboarding phenomenon fully one must also try to understand something of the sport and its associated culture. Its origins lie in surfing and the sunny climes of California and Australia. Its development is due to the invention of the urethane wheel and the independently suspended 'truck' or steering system, and its upsurge in Britain represents its claim to be the first totally urban sport – the response of youth to the concrete jungle. The culture of skateboarding is that of the young: the majority of participants are between 10 and 18 and they identify with the free-wheeling image of surfing and skateboarding. Allied to this in the UK is the current 'punk' revolution with its disenchantment with society which has tended to bring skateboarders into confrontation with authority. This has, however, had other implications in that skateparks have often become centres for a total youth culture and have provided venues for pop concerts,

exhibitions and socialising for young people. However, people who had visited skateparks have generally been impressed with the discipline of skateboarders and their concentration on skateboarding while participating.

The activity, if it is to be classified as a true sport, will need to have a number of competitive disciplines. At the moment these are:

1 Slalom – which may be standard slalom as described above; ramp slalom, which uses a ramp to produce acceleration and cones on a flat area; or giant slalom, which is done in a 'snake' run over a greater distance.
2 Speed – which requires the skater to go as fast as possible over a known distance downhill.
3 Freestyle – which involves the performance of tricks on a flat area.
4 Bowl riding – which involves technique in the riding of bowl runs.

For the purpose of record-making, high jump and long jump skateboarding, clearing heights and distances from one skateboard to another are also recognised.

The control of the sport is now in the hands of the Skateboard Association, whose responsibility it is to establish rules for competition, qualifications for coaching and generally to act as the controlling body for the sport in the UK. This will provide a greater degree of organisation for the sport than has so far been apparent and also a co-ordinating body to act on behalf of clubs and skateboarders. Organisations contemplating the provision of facilities are advised to contact the Association for advice.

Recommended reading
London Topics No 24, *Skateboarding*, free from the Greater London Council, Information and Library Services, Director General's Department, Room 514, County Hall, London SE1 7PB
TUS Data Sheets 19 and 20, *Facilities for Skateboarding*, free from the Sports Council, 70 Brompton Road, London SW3 1EX. The Skateboard Association is at the same address.
Report of a Seminar on Skateboarding, 50p from the Scottish Sports Council, 1–3 St Colme Street, Edinburgh EH3 6AA
The Skatekats Safety Guide, from the Royal Society for the Prevention of Accidents, Cannon House, The Priory Queensway, Birmingham B4 6BS
Safe Skateboarding – A Guide, from the Skateboard Association
There are a number of monthly skateboarding magazines. Four of the most popular are *Skateboard*, *Skateboard Special*, *Skateboarders* and *Skateboard Scene*.
There are also a very large number of books on skateboarding, mainly aimed at participants. The British Safety Council recommends *Skateboard Manual*, published by Theorem Publications Limited at 60p.

Another small-scale installation at Croydon Skatepark (left) this time a 'half pipe' unit. This sort of equipment can be used indoors as well as outside, increasing its amenity value. Large outdoor skateparks do, however, provide more room for open bowls, though 'drop bowls' can be constructed indoors.

DESIGN COUNCIL.

Sources of further information

Two related Design Council catalogues, *Street furniture* and *Equipment for parks and amenity areas*, are being published at the same time as this book. Each catalogue lists a wide range of well designed equipment with complete technical specifications, and many products are illustrated. All products listed have been chosen for their high standard of design by the Design Council's independent Street Furniture Advisory Committee. The members of the Committee are

Neville Conder FRIBA AADipHons FSIAD
Casson Conder & Partners

A J Cryer FICE FIMunE MIHE
City Engineer
Westminster City Council

Jack Howe RDI FRIBA PPSIAD
Consultant Designer

Michael Middleton CBE FSIAD HonFRIBA
Director, Civic Trust

R Robson-Smith FRIBA
Chief Planning Architect
Greater London Council

Bruce Watkin MRTPI
Deputy Secretary
Royal Fine Art Commission

Peter Dawson MSIAD
Design Council

Both catalogues should be of considerable assistance in creating streets and parks that are a pleasure to use, from both a practical and a visual standpoint. The following list gives the names of manufacturers featured in the catalogues, which are available from the Design Centre Bookshop, 28 Haymarket, London SW1Y 4SU. *Street Furniture* costs £10.00 (plus £1.00 postage and packing) and *Equipment for parks and amenity areas* costs £7.50 (plus 80p postage and packing).

USEFUL ORGANISATIONS

Arboricultural Association
incorporating the Association of
British Tree Surgeons and Arborists
Brokerswood House
Brokerswood
Nr Westbury
Wilts BA13 4EH

Architectural Heritage Fund
Civic Trust
17 Carlton House Terrace
London SW1Y 5AW

Association for the Protection
of Rural Scotland
20 Falkland Avenue
Newton Mearns
Renfrewshire G77 5DR

Association of Public Lighting Engineers
Buckingham Court
78 Buckingham Gate
London SW1E 6PF

The Brick Development Association
Woodside House
Winkfield
Windsor, Berks SL4 2DP

British Cycling Bureau
Stanhope House
Stanhope Place
London W2 2HH

British Standards Institution
2 Park Street
London W1A 2BS

Cement & Concrete Association
Wexham Springs
Slough, Bucks SL3 6PL

Centre for Environmental Studies
62 Chandos Place
London WC2N 4HH

Chartered Institute of Transport
80 Portland Place
London W1N 4DP

The Chartered Institution of
Building Services
49 Cadogan Square
London SW1X 0JB

Civic Trust
17 Carlton House Terrace
London SW1Y 5AW

Committee for Environmental Conservation
29 Greville Street
London EC1N 8AX

Council for the Protection of Rural England
4 Hobart Place
London SW1W 0HY

Council for the Protection of Rural Wales
Cymdeithas Doigelu Harddwch Cymru
14 Broad Street
Welshpool
Powys SY21 7SD

Countryside Commission
John Dower House, Crescent Place
Cheltenham, Glos GL50 3RA

Design Council
28 Haymarket
London SW1Y 4SU

Georgian Group
2 Chester Street
London SW1X 7BB

The Landscape Institute
12 Carlton House Terrace
London SW1Y 5AH

National Playing Fields Association
25 Ovington Square
London SW3 1LQ

Northern Ireland Sports Council
49 Malone Road
Belfast BT9 6RZ

Pedestrians' Association for Road Safety
1/4 Crawford Mews
York Street
London W1H 1PT

Planning Exchange, Scotland
186 Bath Street
Glasgow G2 4HG

Royal Fine Art Commission
2 Carlton Gardens
London SW1Y 5AA

Royal Fine Art Commission for Scotland
22 Melville Street
Edinburgh EH3 7NS

Royal Institute of British Architects
66 Portland Place
London W1N 4AD

The Royal Town Planning Institute
26 Portland Place
London W1N 4BE

Scottish Civic Trust
24 George Square
Glasgow G2 1EF

Scottish Design Council
72 St Vincent Street
Glasgow G2 5TN

Scottish Georgian Society
5B Forres Street
Edinburgh EH3 6BJ

Scottish Sports Council
1 St Colme Street
Edinburgh EH3 6AA

Sports Council
70 Brompton Road
London SW3 1EX

Sports Council for Wales
National Sports Centre for Wales
Sophia Gardens
Cardiff CF1 9SW

Victorian Society
1 Priory Gardens
London W4 1TT

Water Space Amenity Commission
1 Queen Anne's Gate
London SW1H 9BT

Index of manufacturers

	1 Co-ordinated street furniture	2 High mast lighting	3 Group A DoT approved lighting columns	4 Group A lighting	5 Group B lighting	6 Shelters and kiosks	7 Poster display units	8 Footbridges	9 Miscellany	10 General lighting	11 Bollards including posts and traffic bollards	12 Litter bins	13 Planting	14 Outdoor seating including tables	15 Guard-rails, parapets, fencing and walling	16 Paving	17 Children's playground equipment
Abacus Municipal Ltd		2	3	4	5	6				10	11	12		14	15		
Adamson Butterley Limited								8									
Anglian Building Products Ltd								8									
The Automobile Association									9								
Barlow, Tyrie Ltd									9			12		14			
Bergo Ltd															15		
William Booth & Co (Metal Work) Ltd				4													
Borer Engineering Co Ltd											11						
Braidholm Engineering Ltd				4													
Brickhouse Dudley Ltd									9				13				
British Aluminium Co Ltd															15		
British Rail Engineering Ltd												12		14			
British Steel Corporation, Tubes Division			3	4	5			8							15		
Brooklyns Westbrick Limited											11				15	16	
W F Broomfield Ltd														14			
Buffalo Fence Ltd															15		
Burnham Signs									9			12					
Burt Boulton (Timber) Ltd								8									
Butterley Building Materials Ltd																16	
Francis Carr																	17
C M Churchouse Ltd										10	11						
Cohen Brothers (Electrical) Ltd				4	5												
Colorguard Ltd															15		
Concrete Utilities Ltd		2	3	4	5				9	10	11	12					
Control Systems Ltd									9								
Albert Cook & Son (Founders) Ltd															15		
J & G Coughtrie Ltd										10							
CU (Bridges) Limited								8									
Eleco Ltd				4	5				9								

Index of manufacturers

1–9 Street Furniture Catalogue only

10–16 Both Catalogues

17 Parks and Amenity Areas Catalogue only

	1 Co-ordinated street furniture	2 High mast lighting	3 Group A DoT approved lighting columns	4 Group A lighting	5 Group B lighting	6 Shelters and kiosks	7 Poster display units	8 Footbridges	9 Miscellany	10 General lighting	11 Bollards including posts and traffic bollards	12 Litter bins	13 Planting	14 Outdoor seating including tables	15 Guard-rails, parapets, fencing and walling	16 Paving	17 Children's playground equipment
E P Plastics Ltd																	17
Esplana Ltd													13				
Eternit Building Products Ltd																16	
Euracel Ltd																	17
Fabrikat Engineering Co Ltd			3	4	5												
George Fischer Sales Ltd									9		11						
Fisher-Karpark Ltd									9								
Furnitubes International Ltd												12		14	15		17
GEC (Street Lighting) Ltd		2	3	4	5					10							
Geometric Furniture Ltd														14			
Glasdon Ltd						6			9		11	12	13				
Green Brothers (Geebro) Ltd												12		14			
Haldo Developments Ltd									9								
Hawsigns Ltd							7										
Hemcol Ltd			3	4	5												
Holophane Europe Ltd					5					10							
Holton Furniture														14			
Ibstock Building Products Ltd																16	
S & D Laycock Engineering Ltd														14			
London & Provincial Posters Limited						6	7										
Marley Buildings Ltd															15	16	
Marlin Lighting										10							
S Marshall & Sons Ltd																16	
Mather & Smith Ltd													13				
A W May Ltd							7										
Metalliform Ltd												12					
Mills & Allen Ltd							7										
Milton Keynes Development Corporation	1					6						12		14			
Mono Concrete Ltd	1						7		9		11	12	13	14	15	16	
Trevor Morrison Ltd											11						
Neptune Concrete Ltd														14			
Norman & Sons (Marketing) Ltd															15		

	1 Co-ordinated street furniture	2 High mast lighting	3 Group A DoT approved lighting columns	4 Group A lighting	5 Group B lighting	6 Shelters and kiosks	7 Poster display units	8 Footbridges	9 Miscellany	10 General lighting	11 Bollards including posts and traffic bollards	12 Litter bins	13 Planting	14 Outdoor seating including tables	15 Guard-rails, parapets, fencing and walling	16 Paving	17 Children's playground equipment
Orchard Seating Ltd												12		14			
Petitjean & Company (UK) Ltd			3	4	5					10							
Philips Electrical Ltd				4													
Phosco Ltd		2		4	5					10							
PJP Trading Ltd														14			
Post Office Telecommunications									9								
Pullen Foundries Ltd													13				
Queensbury Signs Ltd							7										
Recticel Ltd																	17
Redland Aggregates Ltd																16	
Rentaplay Ltd														14			
Roto-Plastic Containers Ltd												12					
Borough of Rushmoor												12					
Sanders Tubecrafts Ltd								8									
Simplex GE Ltd					5					10							
Sinclair (Contract Furnishers) Limited						6											
Sloan & Davidson Ltd													13				
SMP (Landscapes) Ltd	1											12		14			17
South Coast Welders Ltd								8									
The Staines Tinware Manufacturing Co Ltd											11						
Stanton & Staveley				4	5												
Street Furniture Ltd									9						15		
Thorn Lighting Ltd			3	4	5					10							
Town & Country Steelcraft Ltd															15		
Townscape Products Ltd	1										11	12	13	14			
UAC International Ltd															15		
UAC Timber (Wragby)															15		
The Universal Parking Meter Co Ltd									9								
Urban Enviroscape Ltd	1					6	7			10		12		14			
VEB Ltd														14			
Venner (see Fisher-Karpark Ltd)									9								
Charles Wicksteed & Co Ltd												12					17

Manufacturers' addresses

Abacus Municipal Ltd
Sutton-in-Ashfield
Notts NG17 5FT

Adamson Butterley Limited
Ripley
Derby DE5 3BQ

Anglian Building Products Ltd
Atlas Works, Lenwade
Norwich NR9 5SW

The Automobile Association
Fanum House
Basing View
Basingstoke, Hants RG21 2EA

Barlow, Tyrie Ltd
Springwood Industrial Estate
Rayne Road
Braintree, Essex CM7 7RN

Bergo Ltd
Otterspool Way
Watford WD2 8HY

William Booth & Co (Metal Work) Ltd
Palatine Works, Causeway Avenue
Warrington WA4 6QQ

Borer Engineering Co Ltd
Stocks Lane, Bracklesham Bay
Chichester, West Sussex PO20 8NT

Braidholm Engineering Ltd
73 Montrose Avenue
Hillington Industrial Estate
Glasgow G52 4NS

Brickhouse Dudley Ltd
Dudley Road West
Tipton, West Midlands DY4 7XD

British Aluminium Co Ltd
Regal House, London Road
Twickenham TW1 3QA

British Rail Engineering Ltd
Railway Technical Centre
London Road, Derby DE2 8UP

British Steel Corporation, Tubes Division
   (for lighting columns)
PO Box 32
Halesowen, West Midlands B62 8RU

British Steel Corporation, Tubes Division
   (for bridges and parapets)
Corby Works
PO Box 101
Weldon Road, Corby
Northants NN17 1UA

Brooklyns Westbrick Limited
1 Market Close
Poole, Dorset BH15 1NH

W F Broomfield Ltd
The Old Bakehouse, Ward Road
Totland Bay, Isle of Wight PO39 OBB

Buffalo Fence Ltd
19 Mill Lane,
Benson, Oxford OX9 6SA

Burnham Signs
Burnham & Co (Onyx) Ltd
Kangley Bridge Road
Lower Sydenham
London SE26 5AL

Burt Boulton (Timber) Ltd
Brettenham House
Lancaster Place
London WC2E 7EN

Butterley Building Materials Ltd
Wellington Street
Ripley
Derby DE5 3DZ

Francis Carr
2 Christ Church Road
London N8 9QL

C M Churchouse Ltd
Lichfield Road
Brownhills
Walsall, Staffs WS8 6LA

Cohen Brothers (Electrical) Ltd
Tetlow Bridge Engineering Works
Waterloo Street
Crumpsall
Manchester M8 6XB

Colorguard Ltd
Dennis Road, Tan House Industrial Estate
Widnes, Lancs WA8 0SH

Concrete Utilities Ltd
Great Amwell
Ware, Herts SG12 9TA

Control Systems Ltd
The Island, Uxbridge
Middx UB8 2UT

Albert Cook & Son (Founders) Ltd
273 Wincolmlee
Hull HU2 0QF

J & G Coughtrie Ltd
Montrose Avenue
Hillington
Glasgow G52 4LZ

CU (Bridges) Limited
Great Amwell
Ware, Herts SG12 9TA

Eleco Ltd
Sphere Works
Campfield Road
St Albans, Herts AL1 5HU

E P Plastics Ltd
152/3 Newport Street
London SE11 6AQ

Esplana Ltd
49 Masons Hill
Bromley, Kent BR2 9HP

Eternit Building Products Ltd
Whaddon Road
Meldreth
Royston, Herts SG8 5RL

Euracel Ltd
Commerce Estate, Kingston Road
Leatherhead, Surrey KT22 7LA

Fabrikat Engineering Co Ltd
Fabenco Works, Urban Road
Kirkby-in-Ashfield
Notts NG17 8AP

George Fischer Sales Ltd
46 Eagle Wharf Road
London N1 7EE

Fisher-Karpark Ltd
Gratrix Works
Gratrix Lane
Sowerby Bridge
West Yorks HX6 2PH

Furnitubes International Ltd
90 Royal Hill
Greenwich, London SE10 8RT

GEC (Street Lighting) Ltd
PO Box 17, East Lane
Wembley, Middx HA9 7PG

Geometric Furniture Ltd
The Old Mill
Shepherd Street
Royton, Oldham
Lancs OL2 5PB

Glasdon Ltd
117/123 Talbot Road
Blackpool, Lancs FY1 3QY

Green Brothers (Geebro) Ltd
Lister Woodcraft Division
Hailsham, East Sussex

Haldo Developments Ltd
2 Fornham Road
Bury St Edmunds
Suffolk IP33 2AH

Hawesigns Ltd
Bereford Avenue
Wembley, Middx HAO 1RX

Hemcol Ltd
Debdale Lane
Mansfield Woodhouse
Notts NG19 9NR

Holophane Europe Ltd
Bond Avenue, Bletchley
Milton Keynes MK1 1JG

Holton Furniture
Holton cum Beckering
Wragby, Lincoln LN3 5NG

Ibstock Building Products Ltd
Ibstock, Leicester LE6 1HS

S & D Laycock Engineering Ltd
Swinnow Lane
Stanningley
Pudsey, West Yorks LS28 7XE

London & Provincial Posters Limited
78/86 Brigstock Road
Thornton Heath, Surrey CR4 7JA

Marley Buildings Ltd
Peasmarsh
Guildford, Surrey GU3 1LS

Marlin Lighting
Merchant Adventurers Group
Hampton Road West
Feltham, Middx TW13 6DR

S Marshall & Sons Ltd
Southowram
Halifax
Yorks HX3 9SY

Mather & Smith Ltd
Brunswick Road
Ashford, Kent TN23 1ED

A W May Ltd
1 Clements Road
East Ham, London E6 2DT

Metalliform Ltd
Chambers Road
Hoyland, Barnsley
South Yorks S74 0EZ

Mills & Allen Ltd
160 Swan Lane
Coventry CV2 4HD

Milton Keynes Development Corporation
Wavendon Tower
Milton Keynes, Bucks MK17 8LX

Mono Concrete Ltd
Wettern House
Dingwall Road
Croydon, Surrey CR9 2NY

Trevor Morrison Engineering Ltd
13 Brecknock Road
London N7 0BL

Neptune Concrete Ltd
Quayside Road
Bitterne Manor
Southampton SO9 4YP

Norman & Sons (Marketing) Ltd
12 High Street
Egham, Surrey TW20 9HD

Orchard Seating Ltd
Orchard House, St Martin's Street
Wallingford
Oxon OX10 0DE

Petitjean & Company (UK) Ltd
Teesside Industrial Estate
Dukes Way, Thornaby
Stockton-on-Tees
Cleveland TS17 9LT

Philips Electrical Ltd
Lighting Division, City House
420–430 London Road, Croydon CR9 3QR

Phosco Ltd
Great Amwell
Ware, Herts SG12 9LR

PJP Trading Ltd
Queensway House, Queensway
Hatfield, Herts AL10 0NP

Post Office Telecommunications
Marketing Department
Room 510, 2–12 Gresham Street
London EC2V 7AG

Pullen Foundries Ltd
60 Beddington Lane
Croydon, Surrey CR9 4ND

Queensbury Signs Ltd
19–21 Brunel Road
East Acton, London W3 7UW

Recticel Ltd
18–22 Summerville Road
Bradford, West Yorks BD7 1PY

Redland Aggregates Ltd
PO Box 1, Barrow-upon-Soar
Loughborough, Leics LE12 8LX

Rentaplay Ltd
Bentalls, Pipps Hill Industrial Area
Basildon, Essex

Roto-Plastic Containers Ltd
King Street, Enderby
Leicester LE9 5NT

Borough of Rushmoor
Municipal Offices
Alexandra Road, Farnborough
Hants GU14 6BW

Sanders Tubecrafts Ltd
Higgins Lane
Burscough, Lancs L40 8JB

Simplex GE Ltd
Groveland Road
Tipton, West Midlands DY4 7XB

Sinclair (Contract Furnishers) Limited
Hendon Works, Carlisle Road
Edgware Road, London NW9 0JB

Sloan & Davidson Ltd
Swinnow Lane
Stanningley
Pudsey, West Yorks LS28 7XE

SMP (Landscapes) Ltd
Ferry Lane, Hythe End
Wragsbury, Staines
Middx TW19 6HH

South Coast Welders Ltd
Lympne, Hythe
Kent CT21 4LR

The Staines Tinware Manufacturing Co Ltd
Langley Road, Staines
Middx TW18 2EJ

Stanton & Staveley
PO Box 72
Nr Nottingham NG10 5AA

Street Furniture Ltd
Horton Road, West Drayton
Middx UB7 8JE

Thorn Lighting Ltd, Street Lighting Division
Thorn House, Upper Saint Martin's Lane
London WC2H 9ED

Town & Country Steelcraft Ltd
Reform Road
Maidenhead, Berks SL6 8DA

Townscape Products Ltd
176 Loughborough Road
Leicester LE4 5LF

UAC International Ltd
UAC Timber Division
UAC House, PO Box 1
Blackfriars Road
London SE1 9UG

UAC Timber (Wragby)
Wragby, Lincoln LN3 5NE

The Universal Parking Meter Co Ltd
Morley Road, Tonbridge
Kent TN9 1RA

Urban Enviroscape Ltd
95 Walton Street
London SW3 2HP

VEB Ltd
Stags End House, Gaddesden Row
Hemel Hempstead, Herts HP2 6HN

Venner
See Fisher-Karpark Ltd

Charles Wicksteed & Co Ltd
Stamford Road Works, Digby Street
Kettering, Northants NN16 8YJ

panter hudspith architects